WITNESSES

STUDIES IN THE GOSPELS

BY

THE MOST REV. ALBAN GOODIER, S.J.

ARCHBISHOP OF HIERAPOLIS

CONTENTS

AUTHOR'S PREFACE

IT will not be difficult to see the common purpose of these Studies.[1] Read only the critics, whether Rationalist or Christian, and it would seem that the Gospels must always be surrounded by at least some element of doubt. Read the Gospels themselves, and they are their own convincing witness. External difficulties can always be raised against them, some of which can never be solved; not because they are insoluble, but because the corresponding external evidence is lost. But such difficulties, at their best or worst, are never more than negative or circumstantial; they do not touch, nor do they usually attempt to touch, the positive truth which the Gospels contain on every page, for one who is willing to see. It has been the writer's aim to illustrate this, by drawing out a few of the threads of the Gospel Witness to itself.

[1] Of the following Studies, the first and fifth have appeared in the *Clergy Review*, the seventh in the *Month*, the last in the *Ecclesiastical Review*. The ninth was read before the More Society, London. For the present collection all have been considerably revised. The author is grateful to the respective editors for permission to reprint them in this volume.

WITNESSES TO CHRIST

I

THE WITNESS OF ST. JOHN THE EVANGELIST

I

JOHN had grown old in the service of his Lord ; John, the disciple whom Jesus had loved. All the others had now passed away, his brother James in Jerusalem, Andrew and Peter, crucified for Him who had been crucified for them ; all had gone to their merited reward. He had lived through it all ; from that first discovery by the Jordan, that memorable day when the Baptist had pointed out to them ' the Lamb of God ', and curiosity had stirred him and Andrew to follow, to those last days when the Church of Christ had become a living body, and had spread over the face of the earth. He could look back on those well-nigh seventy years, and see everything now in its right perspective ; he could read the story as a single whole. He could blend the joys with the sorrows, the failures with the successes, the prophecies with their fulfilment, the growth, in spite of every opposition, from the tiny seed into a mighty tree, that proved the life, more than natural, within. He had watched that tree spread its branches from one land into another, and there cast its seed and take root again ; he had seen it pass from Jew to Gentile, eastward to Persia and India, westward from Asia to Greece and Africa, and imperial Rome, and Spain, and the islands at the end of the earth. Everywhere it had found a home, nowhere a soil in which it could not thrive ; it had engrafted upon itself every race of man, made its own the varied lives they lived, and made its life theirs. He would lift up his eyes in thanksgiving for the proofs he had witnessed of the love and devotion of men for his Beloved ;

the trials that had been endured, the blood that had been poured out in torrents, the love that had grown of the brethren for one another, proving how indeed they had passed from death to life.

All this and more the old man had beheld, and he knew that the same would go on for ever ; of the kingdom that had been founded there would be no end. Still there were certain things about which he feared ; for John, the Son of Thunder, had always seen the evil alongside of the good, and even from his youth it had stirred him, so that he had needed to be restrained. As the truth had passed from nation to nation, it had come to be expressed in many tongues ; as it had encountered various atmospheres it had taken on new clothing. There had been those, like the beloved and self-sacrificing Paul, whose fertile brain had found new ways of portraying the oneness of the living Christ ; there had been those who, like Simon Peter, had brought home to men His influence on their ordinary lives. Yet there had been others, less in touch with the original revelation, who in their zeal had wandered a little from the truth ; already there were those within the Church who, if they were not guided wisely, might lead the way to false-hood, might loosen the bond that made them all one. But most of all there were men outside the fold who, if they were left unchallenged, if a firm stand were not made against them, might one day work havoc among the children of God ; able men, whose talents and learning gave them an influence and even an authority of a kind ; philosophising men, with a long tradition of the schools of wisdom behind them ; sympathetic-minded men, awake to every new thing, who welcomed with delight every fresh expression of truth, whether it were the truth or not, who sought to harmonise one expression with another, to renew the old in the language of the new.

Against these last in particular it was needful that there should be some safeguard ; not only for the sake of the simple and unlearned, who could not know the signifi-cance of what they said, but that these same jugglers with words might be protected against themselves and their own subtleties. These men had their own language, as all the sciences had them ; the words they used need not be re-jected, for the teaching of truth no words in any language need be rejected. Still it was necessary that they should be understood and used aright, and John would set himself the task of defining them. These philosophising men thought and revelled in abstract ideas, in universal concepts; if care were not taken these abstractions might oust and usurp the place of the great reality that had been revealed. Jesus was no abstraction, the idea of Jesus had sprung from no human brain. He was a reality, a concrete fact. Yet there was danger lest, in the subtle minds of these philosophers, the fact of Jesus might be accepted, and approved, and even preached, as a beautiful dream, a fascinating myth, a vivid figure of speech, that set in a new light all that they had taught in their tradition and no more. There was danger lest Jesus, and all that He had lived and died for, might be made by these men no more than a further advance along the line of philosophic discovery. Jesus the divine, the successor of the divine Plato; Jesus the source of light and life, as so many had been hailed in Athens and Alexandria before Him; Jesus the Son of God, one more of the sons of the gods who had blessed the world with their gifts since Prometheus had brought down fire from heaven and had given it to men; —in parallels and interpretations like these, more than in all persecutions, and contempt, and opposition, John foresaw the dangers that most would threaten the progress of the truth in the generations that were to come after.

Therefore, before all else, as he wrote his last will and testament, the old man, the last of the witnesses, must make clear, for all posterity to remember, the fact, as opposed to its interpretation only, of the coming of the true Son of God into the world, and its significance to men. They were talking much in the schools of Alexandria of the 'mind' of God, of the 'word' of God as the expression of that mind, of Jesus of Nazareth who had received that 'word', and had revealed it in Himself, in His teaching, in His life, in His very being. Well, if they would so speak let them do so; but let them accept all the consequences. Let them not forget that as God was infinite, so also was the mind of God infinite; that as the mind of God was eternal, so also was the expression of that mind; that if Jesus the Christ was its perfect expression, then was He more than just Jesus of Nazareth, who had been inspired, like some Hebrew prophet or some Delphic priestess, with a divine afflatus. The Word of God, God's

perfect expression of Himself, was with God from all
eternity, the Word of God was inseparable from God Himself ; if Jesus Christ was that Word, then He, too, was by
His very nature with God, and in God, and one with God,
before His birth, before the beginning of the world.
Before Jesus was yet Jesus, He was the Word ; and if He
was the Word, He was God. John begins to write. He
intends to put on record some things which his pre-
decessors, Matthew, Mark, and Luke, have passed over.
But before he will speak of any single event, instinctively,
mindful that there would be admirers of Jesus who nevertheless fail to understand Him, he must first insist on this
basic truth, without which all the rest he would say would
be meaningless.

> In the beginning was the Word
> And the Word was with God
> And the Word was God
> He was in the beginning
> With God.

Let men but bear this in mind, and there would be
much they might say with truth concerning Jesus the Word
of God. He was born in time, yet in Himself He was
beyond all time. He had deigned to become a creature,
human ; He had

> Become in all things like to man
> Without sin ;

He had

> Annihilated himself
> Made obedient
> Unto death
> Even to the death of the cross,

as his friend Paul had strongly but beautifully said ; yet
was He none the less the Source of all creaturehood, the
Container of all creatures, seeing that He was the true
Mind, the Word of the Creator, from whom all creatures
came.

> All things were made through him
> And without him was made nothing
> That was made.

None more than John emphasised the living fact of Jesus Christ the living Man ; none more than he loved Him, as man loves his fellow-man ; yet none more than he, with the clear vision of the mystic who sees through the body of this death, proclaimed the Godhead, absolute and without equivocation, of the Man he loved and had ' handled.'

> That which was from the beginning
> Which we have heard
> Which we have seen with our eyes
> Which we have looked upon
> And our hands have handled
> Of the word of life
> For the life was manifested
> And we have seen
> And do bear witness
> And declare unto you the life eternal
> Which was with the Father
> And hath appeared to us.

' The word of life—the life eternal ! ' This was the next thing John would have posterity not to forget. There were two favourite words often on the lips of Jesus his Beloved, both when He spoke of Himself, and when He spoke of that which He had come on earth to do : ' life ' and 'light '. Jesus, the Word of God ; Jesus, living with the very life of God ; Jesus, come into this world of groping, of life that was not life, that He might refashion it and make it truly live ; Jesus, the life of men if they would have Him ; Jesus, the awakening of men if they would hear Him ; Jesus, the light of men, opening out new vistas, new horizons, that stretched on beyond this world into eternity, even to the very throne of the Father : —this was the Jesus he had come to know, and he longed that the knowledge should not be dimmed. Let the philosophers argue and analyse as they might, but let them not forget that, in the last resort, Jesus was a light that was beyond all philosophy. Let science search and prove, but let it remember that Jesus was a life it could never hope to reach, transcendently above it. John had watched philosophy and science in their seeking, he had seen them apparently content with the results they had attained though they were but the finding of new words ; yet also he had seen that they were not content, and never would be. It was all well enough ; but there was a light and a life beyond all their conclusions, which must on no account be lost from sight or set aside.

In him was life
And the life was the light of men
And the light shineth in the darkness
And the darkness did not destroy it.

———————

That was the true light
Which enlighteneth every man
That cometh into this world.

II

Indeed John knew what it was that he wished to declare ; and we can feel him straining to express his certainty of it, no matter what more subtle men than he might have to say. They were Greeks, skilled in word and argument ; he was but a Jew, trained in no school of dialectics, not even in that hair-splitting method of the Jewish masters, and he could only utter plainly what he knew to be the truth. They could speak with the gathered human wisdom of ages ; he was but a mystic, steeped only in the language of the Hebrew prophets, whose vision, nevertheless, reached beyond their logic, whose certainty was greater than the result of any reasoning, and he could do no more than tell these masters of words what he knew to be the truth. He could only repeat it, with an emphasis which should carry conviction, and then, if they would, let them discover for themselves, by experience of their own, the joy of the revelation.

That which we have seen
And have heard
We declare unto you
That you also may have fellowship with us
And our fellowship may be with the Father
And with his son Jesus Christ
And these things we write to you
That you may rejoice
And your joy may be full

And this is the declaration
Which we have heard from him
That God is light
And in him there is no darkness.

What a contrast was this to the idea of the gods they
professed to serve, if indeed they still made any profession
of service of the gods at all ! Their ' unknown ' gods, their
gods who taught them nothing, who lived their lives apart
and aloof on high Olympus, caring for man no more than
man himself cared for his beast. He recalled that memorable day, the last during the Feast of Tabernacles in
Jerusalem, when the Temple and the city had been gay
with many lights, and, in accordance with His wont, Jesus
had turned the whole scene upon Himself:

Again therefore
Jesus spoke to them saying
I am the light of the world
He that followeth me
Walketh not in darkness
But shall have the light of life.

He recalled the sharp contrast made by the prophet, the
favourite prophet of the Master, between the darkness that
comes from the science of this earth, and the light that
comes from Him.

They shall look to the earth
And behold trouble and darkness
Weakness and distress
And a mist following them
And they cannot fly away from their distress.

But let them only lift up their eyes and a vision is before
them:

The people that walked in darkness
Have seen a great light
To them that dwell
In the region of the shadow of death
Light is risen.

For a child is born to us
And a son is given to us
And the government is upon his shoulder

And his name shall be called
Wonderful, Counsellor,
God the Mighty
The Father of the world to come
The Prince of peace
His empire shall be multiplied
And there shall be no end of peace
And he shall sit upon the throne of David
And upon his kingdom
To establish it and strengthen it
With judgement and with justice
From henceforth and for ever
The zeal of the Lord of hosts will perform this.

Such was the boon which the coming of the Word into the world would mean, if only the world would accept it. But would it do so ? John looked again into the past and the sight did but make him the more anxious for the future. Jesus had come, and He had not been recognised. Even His own people, who had been trained through the centuries to look for Him, in the end had failed ; what then would be His lot among those who had had no training, who were content with the dim twilight in which they lived ?

He was in the world
And the world was made by him
And the world knew him not
He came unto his own
And his own received him not.

Again and again in His lifetime Jesus Himself had complained of the refusal of men to believe in Him ; from the first His heart had been broken because they would not take the life and the light that He offered to them.

This is the judgement
Because the light is come into the world
And men loved darkness
Rather than the light
For their works were evil
For everyone that doth evil
Hateth the light
And cometh not to the light
That his work may not be proved.

John would not dwell upon it now ; the proofs of rejection were abundant, and again and again he would come back upon them in the Gospel he was about to write. The star had appeared in the East, as Matthew had recorded, and ' the chief priests and scribes of the people ' in Jerusalem had rightly interpreted it ; yet had they not gone to seek the Child that was born, the Son that was given. Signs had been shown to them in plenty ; nevertheless they had always asked for more, they had always found reason to doubt. Some had known in their hearts and had believed ; still, for fear of the consequences, they had dared to go no further. He recalled that final scene of all in the Temple court, when Jesus had made His last appeal :

Jesus therefore said to them
Yet a little while the light is among you
Walk whilst you have the light
That the darkness overtake you not
And he that walketh in darkness
Knoweth not whither he goeth
Whilst you have the light
Believe in the light
That you may be children of light.

Yet to that appeal he could remember only the sad, weakling response ; that though

Many of the chief men also believed in him
(Still) because of the Pharisees
They did not confess him
That they might not be cast out of the synagogue
For they loved the glory of men
More than the glory of God.

So it had been, even when the Light had been visible to the naked eye; so, John knew, it would be in the future, for the nature of man would not change. There would always be Pharisees to be feared ; there would always be the social synagogue, from which to be ostracised would to some be worse than death ; there would always be those who believed in Him but would not confess Him, lest the great ones of the earth contemn them, lest society reject them.

But there was another side to the picture, and to this, rather than to the first, John at this moment would turn his eyes. If in His lifetime most men had passed Jesus by, yet had they not all ; if in the future most men would find other things with which to preoccupy themselves, still there would always be some who would, at whatever cost, receive the light and the life. The advent of Jesus had not been in vain ; come what might, His kingdom would endure for ever, members would continue to enter it, and mankind, on earth as well as in eternity, would be saved from itself by means of that kingdom. Men would continue to be born into the world, and then, through Jesus, the Life, would be born again. Jesus had said it many times, Paul had made it a special theme of his teaching, Peter had dwelt upon it as the crowning of all else, John himself had meditated on it all through the years, and had made it his one invincible joy and encouragement:

As many as received him
He gave them power
To be made the sons of God
To them that believe in his name
Who are born
Not of blood
Nor of the will of the flesh
Nor of the will of man
But of God.

Behold what manner of charity
The Father hath bestowed upon us
That we should be called
And should be
The sons of God
Therefore the world knoweth not us
Because it knew not him
Dearly beloved
We are now the sons of God
And it hath not yet appeared what shall be
We know
That when he shall appear
We shall be like to him
Because we shall see him as he is
And everyone that hath this hope in him
Sanctifieth himself
As he also is holy.

This, then, was the fundamental truth to which John

with his last breath would bear witness, and which, whatever else were forgotten or recalled, he would have his
' little children ' never forget. Jesus, the very Word of
God, had come into the world, had made Himself in all
things like to men :

The Word was made flesh.

Jesus, the Word of God, truly God made truly man, had
lived a life like that of any other man, bearing man's
sorrows and carrying man's griefs:

And dwelt among us.

Jesus, God made man, while living as man, had revealed
Himself to those who had eyes to see, till in the end He had
stood before them as truly the Son of the Father :

And we saw his glory
The glory as it were of the only begotten of the Father
Full of grace and truth.

III

The revelation had grown with time. It had not been,
for most, the discovery of a moment, as it seemed to have
been with his friend, Paul. It had not come as the fruit of
mere devotion ; it had been forced upon those whose eyes
were disposed to see and whose ears were disposed to hear,
who had the light of love unfeigned to guide them. John
could look back over half a century, and recognise how, for
him in particular, step by step the truth had become plain.
He could recall that first day when the Baptist had revealed
Him, and he, with Andrew, had gone after Him, and Jesus

Turning and seeing them follow him
Saith to them
What seek you ?
Who said to him
Rabbi
Where dwellest thou ?
He saith to them
Come and see
They came
And saw where he abode
And they stayed with him that day.

It had all been very ordinary ; they could not have said

what had affected them ; and yet they had come away saying :

We have found the Messias.

He remembered that other occasion, at Cana in the early months, when Jesus

Manifested his glory
And his disciples believed in him ;

though what it was they believed they could not well have said. And again that day by their homes on the shore of the lake of Galilee, when He had passed him by and his brother James, and had shown them special regard and called them :

And they forthwith
Left their nets and father
And followed him.

He could not forget that solemn moment, on the mountain-side above Capharnaum, when Jesus had ' spent the night in the prayer of God ', and had then come down to the multitude, and chosen the Twelve, ' whom he would himself ', and he, John, had been one of them. Nor could he lose the memory of that other day when, returning to the city from over the lake, as if for a new campaign, He took with Him Simon, and James, and himself, apart even from the rest of the chosen Twelve, and raised a child to life before their eyes. Thus He had shown them His power that they might grow in trust of Him ; later He had shown in turn He trusted them. He had sent them out to preach in His stead ; He had given them His own gift of miracles, in His name they had cast out devils and done other wonders.

But of all those days of activity none stood out more in the memory of John than that solemn day in the synagogue of Capharnaum, when for the first time Jesus had spoken to them all of the Bread of Life. That had indeed been a wonderful day ; a day at once of revelation and testing. When men had turned away and had walked with Him no more, because, at last, He had said what they would not receive ; when at the end Jesus had looked on His own and had asked them :

Will you also go away ?

John's whole heart had followed the words of Simon's spontaneous reply :

Lord
To whom shall we go ?
Thou hast the words of eternal life.

On that day, under that testing, of faith and love combined,—for what but love could have led to such an act of faith ?—the die had been cast ; from that day all the rest had followed, as it were by the ordinary course of natural development. When, some months later, Jesus had put them to the further test, and had asked them :

Whom do you say
That I am ?

and Simon had again spontaneously answered for them all :

Thou art the Christ
The Son of the Living God ;

none more than John had known and understood the significance of the declaration, and had echoed it with all his soul. ' The Christ, the Son of the Living God.' More than once words like these had been used before ; now and henceforth they were to have their full meaning, and the Son of Thunder would have it proclaimed without qualification, through all the generations to come. A week later Jesus had been transfigured, again in the sight of His chosen Peter, and James, and himself ; and John again knew that this was but a confirmation of the faith they had professed. It is true he had still remained the human being that he was, with his native vehemence and sense of justice. He had still protested against some who cast out devils in the name of Christ without due authority ; he had still been roused to indignation when mere Samaritans treated his Master with contempt ; he had still fostered high ambitions, reaching up he knew not whither. But for all his short-comings the heart of John had loved much ; more and more it had been fixed on its Beloved, until there was nothing that could tear them apart.

So John had grown in love during those two years, and love had clarified his understanding. It had taught him the depth of meaning that lay beneath the words, so often on the Master's lips, ' life ', and ' light ', and ' sonship ' ; when such a Lover used them, what limit could be put to

their content ? He could look back now and see what his
Lord had meant when He had replied to his mother's
ambitious request:

> You shall indeed drink of the chalice
> That I drink of
> And with the baptism wherewith I am baptised
> You shall be baptised
> But to sit on my right hand
> Or on my left
> Is not mine to give you
> But to them for whom it is prepared
> By my Father.

When, only a few days later, he alone of the Twelve had
stood beneath a cross on Calvary with the Mother of the
Lord, and had received from Him a gift, the like of which
was given to no other, then he had the key to the meaning
of that promise.

> After that he saith to the disciple
> Behold thy mother
> And from that hour
> The disciple took her to his own.

Yes, indeed,

> Of his fulness we have all received
> And grace upon grace ;

and none could fathom better than John the overflowing
torrent of that divine generosity. It was a great thing to
have been of the Chosen People, born a son of Abraham,
trained in the obedience of the Law ; but this new gift,
given at such a moment, transcended all the rest :

> For the law was given by Moses
> (But) by Jesus Christ came grace and truth ;

and whatever else John might leave behind him for the
guidance of the ages to come, to this solemn certainty he
would witness above all the rest.

> These things are written
> That you may believe
> That Jesus is the Christ
> The Son of God
> And that believing
> You may have life
> In his name.

Last of all, with all his mysticism, and with all that swinging to and fro of his language to which love alone gives the key, John is found to be no less practical in his outlook than are Peter, and James, and Paul. Not for nothing, even if life on this earth alone be considered, had Jesus Christ, the Word, the true Son of God, come into this world. He had come that this material world might be the better for His coming ; indeed how could a world but be better which the feet of the God-man had trod ?

For this purpose the Son of God appeared that He might destroy the works of the devil. He had come, first, that sin, the evil of man's own doing, might be forgiven, and eliminated, and that the wound might be healed :.

> If we walk in the light
> As he also is the light
> We have fellowship with one another
> And the blood of Jesus Christ
> Cleanseth us from all sin.

He had come, next, that in the place of mutual antagonism, hitherto the basis of history, there should reign in the world love of man for man, as man's principle and guide :

> For this is the declaration
> Which you have heard from the beginning
> That you should love one another ;

and when John touches on this last he can scarcely leave it alone. It is the sign of true discipleship, it is the ideal of all likeness to Jesus, it is the one commandment He has left behind, the one manifestation of true faith

> In this we have known the charity of God
> Because he hath laid down his life
> For us
> And we ought to lay down our lives
> For the brethren.

> And whatsoever we shall ask
> We shall receive of him
> Because we keep his commandments

And do those things which are pleasing in his sight

And this is his commandment
That we should believe
In the name of his son Jesus Christ
And love one another
As he hath given commandment unto us.

This, then, is the witness of John, the disciple whom Jesus in some special way had loved. He had seen and believed, a phrase he uses more than once, and he knew that Jesus had in very deed proved Himself to be truly God. No twisting of words, no accommodation, not even for the sake of peace in the schools, must be allowed to alter this fundamental fact ; no specious constructing of philosophy or science must be allowed to explain it away. It stood out alone among all the facts in this world's chronicle ; now revealed, it was the beginning of a new era for the human race, a new light, a new life, a new relation between God and man, and between every man with every other ; an era in which man would be, no longer merely God's creature, but in very truth His adopted son, in which men would be, no longer rivals on an unending battlefield, but brethren in a common Father's house :

Behold the tabernacle of God with men
And he will dwell with them
And they shall be his people
And God himself with them shall be their God.

Upon that truth the future world was to be built ; a world in which sin was to find its antidote, in which love of men for one another was to be a new bond uniting them together, in which peace among men was to be made secure. The one was the outcome of the other. If John, as he did, taught so vehemently the love of men for one another, it was because he saw, with the vision that was more than that of men, that it rested, and could only rest, on the knowledge and love of Jesus Christ, the true Son of God.

THE WITNESS OF ZACHARY

I

THERE was a sullen peace hanging over Jerusalem in the days when Herod was king in Judæa. He was no proper Jew, yet would he pass for one, and his Jewish people resented it. By nature and life he was the cruellest of men, yet would he act the part of a lover of the Law, and his subjects bore it with a sneer. Priests and lay-folk alike must obey him ; yet would he be known to posterity as the rebuilder of the Temple and the restorer of its rites and customs. Hence it came about that in his time, in spite of Roman conquest and desecration, in spite of the falling away of many, to whom the Law was a bond of union and no more, the life in the Temple was nevertheless vigorous and active. The Pharisees and scribes, the priests and the readers of the Law, the doctors and the schools, flourished in the courts about the Holy Place ; indeed, like Herod, and with him as their pattern, they were absolute in their own field. The ceremonies of the Law were meticulously observed, the feasts of the Law were celebrated with the fullest ceremonial ; a stranger might come into Jerusalem in the days of Herod, and might be struck by the devotion it displayed. He might well have believed that this city of the Jews, this Holy City, this City of David, was by far the most sacred spot in all the world.

But not all the Pharisees and priests were of the same mind with Herod, or were content with that ceremonial religion into which the service of Jehovah had hardened. We have abundant evidence that there were many, both among the higher ranks and among the people, whose faith in God, and in the promises He had made, was always alive and burning. They obeyed the dispensers of the Law, because obey they must ; they observed the ceremonies with the multitude, but in a very different spirit. While the leaders worshipped, and made others worship, to their own personal gain and honour, these worshipped, waiting and longing for the day of liberation to come. They studied the Law and practised it, but did not forget its spirit, and the message for the future it contained ; the words of the prophets, and the prayers of longing in the sacred books, were ever in their hearts and on their lips. Indeed, for those whose faith was true, the very plight in which the children of Israel were then placed made them pray and long the more. For, in spite of the show of devotion, and in spite of the contentment of the priests with their lot, was there ever a time when they were more reduced ? Even in the days of the Captivity, at least it was in a foreign land that their forefathers had endured their shame; now it was in their own country, within the walls of their sacred Temple. Here this strange monster ruled over them ; he was king where David had once ruled ; he was the proud lord of the holy place where once Solomon had offered himself and his people to the service of the Lord, and had been received and blessed. Their plight could not be worse, therefore the time for delivery was at hand ; soon He would come who was to be the salvation of Israel.

Thus many in and around Jerusalem prayed in these days, in sadness yet in hope, secretly among themselves, saying little but well understanding one another. The great world, political and religious, might whirl around and above them and they conformed to its demands ; but underneath they lived their own lives, those lives which in all time have made the world's history, though historians must pass them by. Among these was an aged couple, a priest and his wife, whose home was away from Jerusalem, in a village hidden among the western hills of Judæa. The priest, a faithful levite, belonged to the eighth course or class of levites, called that of Abia, and his name was Zachary ; his wife, Elizabeth, was also of priestly descent, being a daughter of the house of Aaron. They were good people ; in their village among the hills they were held in respect, first because of their priestly origin and rank, but also because of what they were ;

Just before God
Walking in all the commandments
And justifications
Without blame.

That is to say, in their observance, both in the synagogue and in the Temple in their careful fulfilment of the requirements of the Law, in prayer, in honesty, and especially in the care of the poor, Zachary and Elizabeth were model Jews in their village home. One only grief beset them, but even to that they had become resigned ; during all the years of their married life God had never blessed them with a child. It was a grief, most of all, because childlessness was held among the Jews to be some kind of disgrace ; if God did not bless a family with children, that family must be unpleasing in some way in His eyes. But even that cross they had learnt to bear ; they were now past sixty, ' well advanced in years,' and they would endure their sorrow together to the end.

Regularly, at the time appointed, Zachary had gone up to the Temple to take his turn in performing the duties of the priesthood. He had joined in the sacrifices, he had looked to the poor, he had offered up the prayer of the ceremonial ; his figure, now grown old in service, was well known on the steps that led up to the Holy of Holies. Regularly, too, on the two occasions in the year when the lot was cast, he had stood with the other priests waiting to see whether at last it would fall to him to enter the Holy Place, and offer the incense that represented the prayer of all the people. But, during all these years, never yet had the lot fallen to him. Not that he looked for it, much less expected it ; a childless man, living away from the ordinary ways of men, coming up to the Temple only when duty called him, he was well content that the honour should fall to others ; for it was an honour that, once received, remained with a priest for the rest of his life. Once only was it permitted to any man ; he who had once entered the Holy Place might never enter it again. Zachary had long become content that younger and better men than he should have the glory, and he should remain unknown.

Yet one day he stands once more with the other priests before the Holy of Holies, waiting for the lot to be cast. The crowd of worshippers is gathered about, offering its prayers and incense, looking to see who will be chosen to enter the Holy Place and present their petitions to the Lord God of Israel. The dawn has appeared in the East over Olivet ; the streak of light has flashed upon the golden pinnacles of the Temple ; the trumpet has sounded the call to prayer ; the chief priest proceeds to choose by lot before the people who their spokesman to the Lord shall this time be. The lot falls on the course of Abia ; in the course of Abia it falls on the old man Zachary ; after all these years of service at last his turn has come to offer on the altar within the Holy Place the incense representing the prayers of Israel. There is joy among the crowd gathered on the spot, for Zachary is beloved among them ; in Zachary's own heart there is an added joy, a sense of reward unlooked-for after these years of fidelity.

Zachary took from the ministering priest the incense that was to be offered ; companions chosen by himself went with him, bearing the fire and what else was needed. The heavy curtains hanging before the Holy Place were lifted and he entered in ; his companions retired and left him' alone in the presence of God. He performed the duty allotted to him ; he burnt the incense on the golden altar ; the smoke went up through the aperture above, and was seen outside ; ' all the multitude were praying without.' Zachary bowed before the Lord, happy in this consolation that had been given to him, as it seemed, at last ; through the long years he had waited and prayed, and though his prayers seemed to have come to nothing, yet this one favour, this moment of close intimacy with the Lord, was an assurance that all was well. He bowed down before God ; he raised himself to depart, stepping backward, for he must not turn his back on the Holy of Holies ; as he did so he became aware that he was not alone, there was another in the Holy Place with him.

> And there appeared to him an angel of the Lord
> Standing on the right side
> Of the altar of incense.

We do not know what form the angels assumed in their many apparitions throughout the Old Testament. To the saints of God the presence of a spirit is more often spiritually than sensibly felt ; how often do they tell us that they ' saw with the eyes of the soul ' ? But the vision is none the less real on that account ; indeed, since the object seen is itself spiritual, it may well be the more real. Be that as it may, Zachary that morning, as he rose from his act of adoration before the altar, knew that on his right, between the golden altar and the seven-branched candlestick, there stood a figure which had not been there before. What it was he did not yet know, but he did know that it was not of this earth. The old man was uneasy ; he could not but wonder what this vision portended, whether it were an omen, good or bad.

> And Zachary seeing him was troubled
> And fear fell upon him.

II

Zachary did not dare to speak. Though his office had been fulfilled and it was time for him to go, though he knew the crowd outside was impatiently awaiting him, and that blessing it was his next duty, he stood fixed to the spot in the Holy Place. At length the figure spoke ; its voice was reassuring, its message was poured out in a very torrent, overwhelming. First it was a message to himself, and to his wife, Elizabeth ; at last, even by miracle, though long since they had ceased to hope, the prayer of their lives was heard. Next it was a message that told of the son that would be given to them, and the kind of man he would one day be. But last, and most important of all, the messenger spoke of the place that son would take in the design of the Lord. At length the time had come, the fulness of time. The Lord Himself was about to appear on the earth, and the son of Zachary would be His herald, His fore-runner, he would be the new Elias.

> And the angel said to Zachary
> Fear not Zachary
> For thy prayer is heard
> And thy wife shall bear a son
> And thou shall call his name John
> And thou shalt have joy and gladness
> And many shall rejoice in his nativity.
> For he shall be great before the Lord
> And shall drink no wine nor strong drink
> And he shall be filled with the Holy Ghost
> Even from his mother's womb.

And he shall convert many of the children of Israel
To the Lord their God
And he shall go before him
In the spirit and power of Elias
That he may turn the hearts of the fathers
Unto their children
And the incredulous to the wisdom of the just
To prepare unto the Lord a perfect people.

The message rang in the ears of Zachary, as it were an answer to his prayer at all points. It grew as his prayer had grown with the years, from those first longings for a son, to the yet greater longing that had followed, for that other Son, that Son of man whom the prophet Daniel had so clearly foretold. It was a message indeed of assurance, of hope and joy, coming from one who was a reader of hearts ; by no other words would the soul of Zachary have been more filled with consolation. In spite of his years and the years of Elizabeth, a son was to be born to them, even by miracle, by the ordination of the Lord. His thoughts went back to that other visit of angels to his father Abraham, when at last he, too, was promised a son, whose posterity would be as the stars in the heavens for number. He remembered Anna and her prayer, at the door of the Tabernacle in Sichem, and how God blessed her with a son, Samuel the last of the patriarchal line, the founder of the line of the Lord's anointed. Zachary was to call his son John, a name that meant ' God giveth grace ' ; not a new name, common enough among the Jewish people, yet this time to have its full significance. He thought back to the others whose names had been given to them for a sign ; to Adam, and Abraham, and Israel, and many of the prophets; and he knew that this, too, was a proof that the son to be born to him would be in the tradition of the patriarchs and prophets of the past. At last, in his son, was to come the great revival, in his son the voice of the prophets was again to be heard ; here was joy and gladness enough for himself, joy in abundance for all those who had waited so long for the revelation.

Moreover, to one steeped in the scriptures, how the words of the heavenly messenger rang with echoes of the patriarchs and prophets of old ! It seemed as if the very essence of the sacred books had been distilled from them, and was being poured out upon the head of the child that was to be, like the oil that was poured on the head of Aaron at his consecration. Like Moses, his child was to be ' great before the Lord '; like the consecrated Nazarites he was to ' drink no wine nor strong drink '; like the prophets he was ' to be filled with the Holy Ghost ', and that, like Samuel, ' even from his mother's womb '. Like Isaias and Jeremias he would ' convert many of the children of Israel to the Lord their God ', nay, he would be the fore-runner of Him that was to come, he would be the Elias returned in his chariot of fire :

He shall go before him
In the spirit and power of Elias.

As if he would link up this new message with all that had gone before, the angel had quoted the very words of the last of the prophets.

Behold I will send you Elias the prophet
Before the coming of the day of the Lord
Great and dreadful
And he shall turn the heart of the fathers
To the children
And the heart of the children
To their fathers
Lest I come
And strike the earth with anathema.

Behold I will send you my angel
And he shall prepare the way
Before my face
And presently the Lord whom you seek
And the angel of the testament whom you desire
Shall come to his temple
Behold he cometh
Saith the Lord of hosts.

This, then, was the son that was to be his own, Elias returned, the angel preceding the advent of the Lord, whose prayer would ascend like that of Elias and would be heard :

> Hear me, O Lord, hear me
> That this people may learn
> That thou art the Lord God
> And that thou hast turned their heart again.

Zachary heard the message and, as each phrase brought back these memories, he realised its significance. But could it be true? How should he know that the vision was no dream, no delusion, no fancy worked up by his own desires? He thought of like scenes in the story of the past; how when a child had been promised to Abraham and Sara in their old age,

> Abraham fell upon his face
> And laughed saying in his heart
> Shall a son thinkest thou
> Be born to him that is a hundred years old?

He thought of the father of Samson, Manue, who had been promised a son and had not known what to believe; of Anna, the mother of Samuel, who had been heard and blessed by Heli the high-priest. True, they had not asked for signs; yet Abraham at least had seemed to doubt. And if to-day, at last, this new revelation was about to dawn, if all the past of the Chosen People had been only one long preparation for this day, would he not be justified in asking for some confirmation of the message? The old man wavered; he was weak and feeble, and his word with those outside would carry little weight; who would believe the message he brought them, unless he had proof in a sign?

> And Zachary said to the Angel
> Whereby shall I know this?
> For I am an old man
> And my wife is advanced in years.

In the Holy Place Zachary had hesitated. Although of the fact of the angel he seems to have had no doubt, he had asked for a further sign. Not so had Abraham done, though he had thought the promise impossible; not so Manue or Anna, though they, too, had wondered how this thing could be. The angel met his request ; with all the dignity that became a messenger of God he presented his credentials. He gave his name ; that should be to him sufficient sign. He was Gabriel, the Power of God ; Gabriel, one of those who stood for ever round the throne of God ; Gabriel, the witness to Daniel of all that was to come in the dispensation of the Lord ; Gabriel, the angel of the Messias. All this would crowd in upon the mind of Zachary at the mere mention of the messenger's name. But since he had asked for a sign he should have one. It should be both a sign and a chastisement, for the right fruit of unfaith was speechlessness. It should be a sign to others as well as to himself ; let them learn from his silence what, perhaps, they would be slow to hear.

And the angel answering said to him
I am Gabriel
Who stand before God
And am sent to speak to thee
And to bring thee these good tidings
And behold thou shalt be dumb
And shalt not be able to speak
Until the day
Wherein these things shall come to pass
Because thou hast not believed my words
Which shall be fulfilled in their time.

The vision was over ; Zachary found himself alone once more in the Holy Place before the altar. Meanwhile in the court outside the crowd of worshippers had begun to grow restless and wondered. The offering of the incense had been a matter of but a few minutes ; they had seen the smoke rise up through the opening in the roof, and there had been no further reason for Zachary to delay. At length he appeared ; the curtain was drawn, and the old man stood in front of them. But what was this ? He made as if he would bless them in the customary form ; he raised his hand to bless, he opened his mouth to pronounce the words, but the words would not be formed. He was not as he had been when he left them ; besides his silence, there was that in his face and eyes which showed that his thoughts were elsewhere. He seemed to see what they did not see ; his silence was as if some sense of awe had made him speechless ; it was not a mere paralysis of the tongue. Clearly while he had been in the Holy Place something unwonted had happened ; God in His own house had in some way shown Himself to Zachary. As he came more to himself, the more he tried to speak, to be as he had been before. It was of no avail, not a word could he frame ; and his friends led him away, pitying his misfortune, wondering what that could be which had brought this distress.

Zachary had still some days to spend at the Temple before the period of his service was done. At last he could retire, back to the village in the hill-country of Judæa from which he had come. He went back to his home, to live and meditate in silence. Elizabeth soon learnt from him what had happened, and the all-important part she was to play ; and she, too, hid herself away, even from her village neighbours, that she might become a worthy mother of the Precursor of the Lord.

And it came to pass
After the days of his office were accomplished
He departed to his own home
And after those days Elizabeth his wife conceived
And hid herself for five months saying
Thus hath the Lord dealt with me
In the days wherein he hath had regard
To take away my reproach from men.

III

We need not delay over the events of the next few months. Elizabeth bore a son in her old age and all the neighbourhood recognised the event as something miraculous.

And her neighbours and kinsfolk
Heard that the Lord had magnified his mercy towards her
And they rejoiced with her.

Eight days more, and the ceremony of circumcision had to be performed, when the child was given his name. By this time it had become a custom among the Jews for the eldest son to take his father's name ; in any case,. names were taken from ancestors in the family. But here the mother interposed. No matter what the relatives might say the child must be called John. There were further protests; the name John was not to be found in all the annals of either family. They appealed to the dumb father ; he called for stylus and tablet, and wrote with emphasis

John is his name.

The rest of the story is told with that vivid simplicity and emphasis which puts St. Luke among the great writers of the world :

And they all marvelled
And at once his mouth was opened
And his tongue loosed
And he spoke, blessing God
And fear fell upon all their neighbours
And throughout the hill-country of Judæa
These things were discussed
And all that heard laid them up in their heart
Saying: What then is this child to be ?
For indeed the hand of the Lord was with him.

Having thus told the whole story of the birth of John, the Evangelist then turns back to give the witness of Zachary, apart and in its completeness. Evidently, to him, it is a crucial passage ; it is the turning-point from the old to the new ; it is the summing up of the past, and the first definite insight into the future. With his own child here before him, and that other child to be born in six short months, Zachary, ' filled with the Holy Ghost ', says St. Luke, pronounces the canticle which has rung through the Church ever since, as the summary of all the history of the dealing of God with men :

And Zachary his father was filled with the
Holy Spirit, and he prophesied, saying
Blessed be the Lord God of Israel,
Because he hath visited and redeemed his people
And hath raised up a Power to save us,
In the house of David his servant,
(As he promised through the mouth of his saints,
His prophets from of old)
To save us from our enemies,
And from the hand of all that hate us.
Thus to show mercy towards our fathers,

And to be mindful of his holy covenant;
Of the oath he swore to Abraham our father,
To grant us that, without fear,
Delivered from the hand of our enemies,
We should serve him in holiness and justice,
Before him, all our days.
And thou, Child, shalt be called Prophet of the Most High,
For thou shalt go before the face of the Lord,
To prepare his ways;
To impart to his people knowledge of salvation,
Through forgiveness of their sins,
By reason of the loving mercy of our God,
Wherewith he shall arise and visit us from on high,
To shine on them that sit in darkness.
And in the shadow of death,
To guide our feet into the path of peace.

Thus the Canticle breaks into two strophes, the one looking to the Messias, and the good thing He bestows, fulfilling the promises of God and the oracles of the prophets; the other describing the function of the child before Him. Zachary begins with the praise and benediction of the Lord, careful to use the formula long consecrated by David, by Solomon, and the long line of psalmists; he blesses the Lord who hath saved His people in the ages past, from the oppression in Egypt, from the captivity in Babylon, and now at last from bondage by His merciful intervention which shall make them free for ever. Now at last, in the name of David, not in his own, the 'house of salvation', the Power that shall finally save, has come into the world, and shall in that same generation be manifested. So the mother of Samuel had sung:

The adversaries of the Lord shall fear him
And upon them shall he thunder in the heavens.
The Lord shall judge the ends of the earth,
And he shall give empire to his king,
And shall exalt the horn of his Christ.

So it had been promised, faithfully and regularly through the ages past, from the days of David His servant, as when Nathan said:

My mercy I will not take from thee,
As I took it from Saul,

Whom I removed from before my face.
Thy house shall be faithful,
And thy kingdom forever before my face,
And thy throne shall be firm forever.

So had proclaimed Isaias, so Jeremias, so Ezechiel, and other prophets. The conqueror would come, the founder of the kingdom of peace wherein God and the King would be served without fear any more from those that serve strange gods, nay, from any enemy whatsoever, whether of this world or not. So will God prove His mercy, the mercy He has promised to the fathers of old, the mercy He has sworn to give to man, as though He would tie His own hands. Though men forget, God has not forgotten ; though the time has seemed long, yet time is as nothing to God ; though the promise is fulfilled to-day, yet have the ages past profited by its fulfilment that was to be. Again and again have the prophets of old sung of the reign of ' holiness and justice without fear ' that was to come. It had come at last ; in the final words of this stanza we hear the dying echo of the songs of Isaias and Jeremias, sung when the people of Israel were in their days of deepest sorrow.

In this way Zachary catches the music of the past centuries, giving it a complete application it had never known before. Now he turns to the child before him, this ' little child ', who nevertheless is one day to be so great. The angel had spoken of him before he was conceived in words that now warrant Zachary in his praise ; the child shall one day be a Prophet, yes, and ' more than a prophet' ; he shall be the one of whom the great prophets themselves have prophesied. He shall go before the face of the Lord ; he shall prepare the world for His immediate coming ; he shall point out for such as will see the way to the kingdom of holiness and justice without fear ; he shall show them the light in its discovery through cleanness of heart. Again Zachary catches the words and spirit of the early prophets ; whatever others may imagine of the kingdom that is to come, Zachary is under no delusions. There is no word of conquest, no word of political domination. As before, he had summed up the past in the mercy of the Lord to the fathers, so now in that same mercy he sees the story of the future.

By reason of the loving mercy of our God, wherewith

He shall rise and visit us from on high, that light that shall shine on them that sit in darkness, that sun of justice, that ' light of the World ', as He shall one day proclaim Himself to be, for Jerusalem, for all men, leading them, if they will follow Him, ' into the path of peace.' Zachary sees well the wide significance of what he is saying. The ' people of Israel ' has grown into the people of the whole world, ' from the rising of the sun even to the setting thereof '. The house of David has been given a son whose kingdom cannot be confined to the land in which David dwelt ; it shall spread across creation, wherever men sit ' in darkness, and in the shadow of death '. Line by line one seems to hear the old man, with his eyes looking into the future, interpreting the prophets who have spoken before him, giving to their words that wider meaning, which the narrow vision of his generation had ignored. Not only, therefore, is the Benedictus of Zachary the link between the Old and the New ; it is also the first charter given to the nations at large, granting them citizenship in the kingdom of Christ.

III

THE WITNESS OF OUR LADY

IT is commonly accepted by students of the Gospels that the first two chapters of the Gospel according to St. Luke come from, and have been virtually dictated by, Our Lady herself. The Evangelist expressly tells us, as if to account for some events which the others do not record, that he has taken his narrative 'from those who from the beginning were eye-witnesses'. He says that he gives it, not on his own authority, nor scarcely in his own words, but 'as it has been delivered unto' him. He says that he has been very careful to get at the exact truth, that he has 'diligently attained to all things from the beginning', and that he writes in order that others may know that truth from its first sources. When, then, he plunges almost at once into the account of the Annunciation, we ask ourselves what other 'eye-witness' was there of that scene but Our Lady, and from whom else could he have received the story? And this all the more since we know from St. Matthew that she concealed it even from St. Joseph. When, immediately after, he relates the story of the Visitation, who but Our Lady could have told him the exact words of the *Magnificat*? And who but she would have been so careful to let him know exactly how long she stayed with her cousin Elizabeth? When he tells of the Nativity, who but a mother would have thought of recording that little detail, almost the only one we know of the event, that 'she wrapped him up in swaddling-clothes, and laid him in a manger', because it was the best thing she could do under the conditions? Then there follow the other scenes, the Loss and Finding of the Child in the Temple, with the concluding statement 'And he went down with them, and came to Nazareth, and was subject to them. And his mother kept all these words in her heart. And Jesus advanced in wisdom, and age, and grace with God and men.' These, and these only, are told us by St. Luke and

by no one else ; and are they not just those things which a
mother would be likely to remember of the early years of
her child ? And are they not told in just a mother's
language, especially the summary at the end ?

Another fact in these two chapters confirms the impression that they have come directly from Our Lady herself ;
it is that through them both she is the prominent character.
We are told things concerning her which no one but herself
could have known, much less would have troubled to
record ; how she ' was frightened ', not at the apparition
of the angel but at his message, and how she ' argued with
herself what on earth it might mean ' ; how on other
occasions she ' kept all these things, pondering them in her
heart ' ; how she ' wondered at the things that were said '.
Last of all, surely no one but Our Lady herself would have
said of her that ' she understood not ' ; she knew so much
more than anyone else ever knew or could know, yet,
because of her knowledge, knew also how much she did
not know.

With good reason, then, many call these two chapters
the Gospel according to Our Lady. And if it is her Gospel,
her own ' good tidings ', one asks oneself whether her
message is in any way new ; whether in any way it differs
from, adds to, what has gone before. Now if we study her
own words, if, for instance, we compare the *Magnificat* with
other like canticles, there is one thing which strikes us at
once. When we look back on the Old Testament, Moses,
the Psalms, the Prophets, we find that their words are
addressed, first of all, to the children of Israel. They are
the Chosen People, they are the heirs of the Redemption,
in them the rest of the world is to be saved. Even when we
come to Zachary, the father of John the Baptist, it is still
the children of Israel that are chiefly considered. Thus he
sings in the Benedictus

> Blessed be the Lord God of Israel
> Because he hath visited
> And redeemed his people
> And hath raised up a Power to save us
> In the house of David his servant.

There is one striking exception ; it is in the Canticle of
Anna (I Samuel ii, 1-10) upon which Our Lady's *Magnificat*

is built.   In the Canticle, though spoken on the eve of the
period of the kings of Israel, no mention is made of the
Israelites apart from anyone else.   The Lord, in this
Canticle, is not only the God of Israel ; He is God of all the
world :

> For the poles of the earth are the Lord's
> And upon them he hath set the world.

Whence the mother of Samuel concludes her Canticle:

> The Lord shall judge the ends of the earth
> And he shall give empire to his kind
> And shall exalt the horn of his Christ.

Still, even with Anna, and with some of the prophets
whose vision also ranges throughout the world, the perspective is measured, as it were, with the eyes of one whose
point of sight is the Temple of the God of Israel.   When
we come to the Canticle of Our Lady it is almost reversed.
It is no longer ' the children of Israel ' that occupy the
centre of the picture, but the whole of the human race.
She glorifies God for what He is, and for what He has
done.   She thanks Him for the great honour He has
bestowed upon her, His hand-maiden ; and the reason is,
not that, like Judith and Esther, she may become another
national heroine, but

> Because from this moment
> All generations shall call me blessed ;

that is, all the race of men shall benefit from the honour
that has been done to her.   In other words, in Our Lady's
' good tidings ', for the first time it would seem, the fruits
of the Redemption are announced to all the world, the
' children of Israel ' are made to include the whole of mankind ;   and she confirms her message by the further
announcement that

> His mercy
> Is from generation unto generations
> To all them that revere him.

Only at the end does she speak of her own people.   This,
she seems to conclude, is the meaning of the prophecies,
and the promises of the Lord God.   Infinite in power,

infinite in mercy, He is the God of all the world, in all place and for all time, and the opening of the floodgates is the special glory of the children of Israel :.

> He hath succoured Israel his servant
> Remembering his mercy
> As he spoke to our fathers
> To Abraham and to his seed
> For ever.

This is the first of the 'good tidings' according to the Gospel of Our Lady ; she and her Son are not for the Jews only but for the whole human race. There is a second which confirms the first. The Jews of her time looked for the Kingdom of this world ; the Messias was to restore the throne of David. Our Lady, too, looks for a kingdom of this world, but of what a different kind ! Though the angel had spoken to her in the language of the prophets, and had described her Son as the ruling successor of David, she knew quite well the wide meaning of his words. Her Son's kingdom would be one, not of might and conquest of other nations, as her people hoped, but one in which

> He hath scattered the proud
> In the conceit of their heart ;

not one in which the victors will lord it over others, but in which

> He hath put down the mighty from their seat
> And hath exalted the humble ;

not a kingdom of wealth and luxury, the only kind of kingdom her generation knew, but in whose realm

> He hath filled the hungry with good things
> And the rich he hath sent empty away.

So different was the kingdom of her Son as Our Lady saw it. Her countrymen viewed it as a conqueror of the world, she saw it as the home of the lowly ; they would proclaim it the seat of the mighty, she beheld only the meek and humble who would inherit the land ; they put their trust in riches, she foretold that in her Son's kingdom it would be those that had nothing who would possess all things.

These, then, would seem to be the two special messages announced in Our Lady's good tidings, caught up from the Canticle of Anna, but refined to the purest gold. The Kingdom to be founded by her Son would be universal ; it would be a Kingdom of the lowly, the meek, the needy, even as were its King and its Queen, who, nevertheless, would have their fill. But once it had been so announced, we find it at once taken up and confirmed by others ; it would almost seem that the angels themselves waited for her to open the new revelation. At the Annunciation the angel Gabriel had spoken only of the kingdom of David and the people of Israel ; now, a few months after Our Lady had spoken, another angel brings the message in very different words. He comes to the shepherds on the hillside and says:

> Fear not
> For behold I bring you good tidings of great joy
> Which shall be to all the people,

not to the children of Israel only ; and he ends his message with the song, taking up the thoughts, and almost the words, of Our Lady herself :

> Glory to God in the highest
> And peace to all on the earth
> Among men of his good pleasure.

Forty days later Our Lady records the meeting with the old man Simeon in the court of the Temple. A year before Zachary had said :

> Blessed be the Lord God of Israel
> Because he hath . . . raised up an horn of salvation
> To us ;

now the aged Simeon proclaims :

> Now thou dost dismiss thy servant, O Lord
> According to thy word in peace
> Because my eyes have seen
> The salvation which thou hast prepared
> Before the face of all peoples.

Before Zachary had spoken of

> The orient from on high
> (that) hath visited us
> To enlighten them that sit in darkness ;

now Simeon, with his new vision, tells us that this will be

> A light to the revelation of the Gentiles

and on that account

> The glory of thy people Israel.

Thus, from the *Magnificat* to the Canticle of Simeon, the air of the Gospel is filled with the light of a new day, seeming to set that section apart from all the rest.   Our Lady and her message have altered the whole of our perspective as to God, and the Kingdom of His Son. But she did not conclude her account of Simeon with this prophecy alone. She had added another ; and this, no less than the first, she had also ' kept in her heart ' through the ensuing years. All these good things were to come to men, salvation for all people, light to all the nations, protection for the lowly, inheritance for the meek, plenty for those in need, but at a price ; and that price her Son, and she herself, were to pay.   First, He would be a sign that would be contradicted ; though He would save many by His coming, yet would many also fall on His account.   And second, her own soul a sword would pierce ; though ' all generations would call her blessed ', yet would she suffer unto death that out of the hearts of many realisation such as this might be revealed.   These were the ' things ' at which, she tells us, she ' wondered ', and which she ' kept in her heart ' through the years, pondering them, seeing their fulfilment in the many events that followed.

For instance when, but a short time later, the children in Bethlehem were put to death on her own Child's account ; she reminded herself that He was ' a sign to be contradicted ', and the thought of the weeping mothers drove the first sword deep into her own mother's heart. When the three homeless strangers wandered in a foreign land, she could not but remember again the ' sign to be contradicted ', and the sword pierced deeper still. And if we go through the rest of the little we know of the life of her Son, with this clue in our hands we may learn much of the still more hidden life of the mother. Wherever we find the sign being contradicted we have but to bear in mind that ' the mother of Jesus was there ', that when He suffered, at that moment, too, the sword pierced her heart, and we shall discover very much about her. She was with Him in Nazareth, and we are expressly told that He took her with Him when He made His home in Capharnaum. Hence in her own city, Nazareth, when the people despised Him because He was only the Son of such a mother, Our Lady looked from her cottage door and the sword went in a little deeper. When on that account they would take Him and do Him to death, she followed the tumult down the street and the sword went deeper still. In Capharnaum the Herodians and Pharisees conspired that they might destroy Him ; she knew what was happening, from the trouble in the streets, from her Son's indignation and vehemence, from her own mother's instinct, and the sword of sorrow pierced her again. So we might go on till Calvary, and there, at last, the supreme sacrifice was made. The sign was contradicted with a final denial, but it was for the resurrection of many ; the sword of sorrow pierced through and could go no further, but, by it, out of many hearts what thoughts have been revealed !

' Mary kept all these things in her heart.' And through all the ages since she has kept them. She who first called down the blessing of her Son on ' all generations ', ' from generation unto generations ', has kept her own words in her heart, and has ever remained ' the handmaid of the Lord ', the channel of His ' mercy ' ; the history of Christendom might be re-written to prove the truth of her prophecy and her care. It is not without a purpose that St. Luke includes her by name with the apostles and disciples at Pentecost, waiting in prayer for the coming of the Holy Ghost ; it was fitting that the Queen of the nations that were to be should be present with these messengers of the Kingdom on the day of their final commission. She was with them then, she has been with their successors ever since. In each generation she continues to prove to her own that she still keeps them in her heart, and, in return, each generation continues to call her blessed, 'Mother of God', 'Help of Christians', 'Immaculate.'

What but this is the significance of Lourdes, the latest of the glories of Mary ? For a century fresh troubles had befallen her beloved mankind, and she would give them proof that she still kept them in her heart. Since then, when old wounds were healed, new troubles have arisen, and she still reminds us, year after year, that she does not forget, she still keeps us in her heart.

> Why do the nations rage ?
> And why do peoples meditate vain things ?

In the midst of the storm Our Lady stands upon the rock, and humility speaks to humility the message that, if men will hear it, will heal this wounded world. She tells a little child that, if the nations will come to her, the proud shall be scattered in the conceit of their hearts, the tyrant shall be put down from his seat, the glutted with wealth shall be sent empty away and instead the hungry shall be filled. This is the abiding miracle of Lourdes, the Gospel of Our Lady brought down to our day, and its fulfilment proved before our eyes. Other miracles she may bestow upon her clients as she will out of her bounty ; they do not demand them, they thank her for them when they come, but they know that they are, what her Son's miracles were, 'signs' and no more. They are the outward signs of that inward grace which she bestows on all the world for its healing. There is pride of life, leading to every other evil and rivalry among nations ; at the feet of Our Lady, for everyone to see who will, all nations are as one. There is untold tyranny and oppression ; about her feet all are equal. There is swollen wealth, with its heel on grinding poverty ; with Mary of Lourdes, who is at once Mary of Nazareth and Mary Queen of heaven, wealth is a word without meaning, poverty is happy and possesses all things.

IV

THE WITNESS OF NAZARETH

I

WE all carry with us to our dying day the impressions of our childhood and youth. Our school days are but an item in our education ; men talk, and act, and legislate as if they were the most important item, but to many, perhaps to most, they are the least. The whole world is our college, our special conditions and circumstances are our class-rooms ; our best teachers are the events of our lives, and the persons we meet every day. Nor does it, nor need it, matter very much in what surroundings we are born ; the lives of the greatest, whether saints or rulers of the world, have begun, perhaps more often than not, in conditions very different from those which men call ideal. All conditions alike have their special training to give ; none are exactly the same, and no amount of legislation, or of social levelling, will make them so. God has His own design as to what He would wish every creature of His hands to be, and He places him where he may be trained for that purpose most perfectly. If He made our early days, and set them in the midst of privation, we know that He has thereby trained us in depth of soul and sympathy ; we see that illustrated again and again in the lives of the saints, and among the suffering poor in our midst. If He has put us into crowded streets, He has given us an early training in the knowledge of men ; if, on the other hand, our lot has been apart, and comparatively easy—for absolutely easy none has been—then there is, or should be, a certain peace and quiet in our nature, which will inevitably show itself in our after lives. If we have grown up in the open country, even in a desert, we have a breadth of vision given to us which may make for greatness, whether in action or in contemplation. Of all the complainings of man none is, usually, less justified than complaining of his lot in life. It does but mean that he has failed to see himself in right perspective ; that he has hidden from himself the good things that have come to him, along with those that he may have thought evil ; that he has overestimated the conditions of others, failing to see that, with or even because of their good fortune, they have not received what he himself has in abundance.

This is true of us all ; in later years, when the lessons of our school days have long been forgotten, we can never forget, or cast aside as outgrown, the lessons our surroundings have taught us. We look back and thank God for many things that have befallen us, many humiliations we shirked at the time, many sufferings and privations we then resented, for now we see what blessings in disguise they were, how they opened our eyes and developed us. We thank Him for many persons that have come across our path and influenced us ; even if we thank Him for the particular place of our education, and for the kind of schooling we have received, more often it is because of its associations, and because of the influences brought to bear upon us, than for the actual instruction we were given. If, on the other hand, we look back on our childhood with regret, usually it is not so much our circumstances as ourselves that we have to blame. No matter where we have been brought up or how, most of us have had our chance if we had chosen to make use of it, if not to be anything in the eyes of men at least to be something in the eyes of God ; those who have had no chance in life are not, usually, those who complain.

If this is true of us all, then there is a sense in which it is true of Jesus Christ Our Lord Himself. We are told of Him that He

> Truly bore our sorrows
> And carried our griefs ;

that

> We have not a high priest
> Who cannot have compassion on our infirmities
> But one tempted in all things
> Like as we are
> Without sin ;

that

> Whereas indeed he was the Son of God
> He learned obedience
> By the things which he suffered ;

that

> The child grew
> And waxed strong
> Full of wisdom,

that

> Jesus advanced
> In wisdom and age and grace
> With God and man.

With this fact so carefully emphasised for us by the Scriptures, we are safe in concluding that the human side of Jesus developed according to His circumstances, and that the surroundings in which He was brought up left their mark upon Him. He was born in Bethlehem of Judæa, He grew to manhood in Nazareth of Galilee ; this made its impression on Him, stamped in a special manner the human way He looked at life, and the human language in which He expressed it. Had He been trained in the crowded streets of Jerusalem, or had He stayed longer years in Egypt, though the revelation of the Good Tidings would have been the same, yet we may be sure it would have been given to us in quite different words, with different illustrations, possibly even in a totally different setting.

For in Nazareth, more perhaps than would have been anywhere else, there were cultivated in Him those ideas, that imagery, which are so strikingly prominent in all His teaching ; to the end of His life Jesus remained a Nazarene. Surrounded by its hills on every side, perched high above the broad valley of Esdraelon, the scene of many a battle in the past ; beyond which rose the mountains of Carmel, and Samaria, and Little Hermon, with the giant sugar-loaf, Thabor, away on the left, Nazareth was a spot to make a thoughtful Jewish boy accustomed to broad visions from high places and to look down from above at the world at large ; it was more than mere caprice that later made the Tempter take Him ' into a very high mountain ' when he wished to try Him with the vision of the whole world at His feet. Again, when, as so often in the midst of His public life, we find Him stealing hours for rest and prayer by hiding Himself in the mountains and lonely places, we cannot doubt that this was no new thing. It was a habit He had learnt in the days of His early training ; in His public life He fled to his beloved mountains, in the morning before the day's work began, in the evening when it was over, even as any hard-worked man will find rest in some familiar haunt of his childhood. Or again when He stood in the streets of Capharnaum, and spoke of

Many (that) shall come
From the east and the west
And shall sit down with Abraham and Isaac and Jacob
In the kingdom of heaven,

we can hear the Man who often in His youth had sat on the ridge that borders Esdraelon, and had watched the caravans passing up and down the valley beneath Him, from Acre and the Roman galleys eastward, or westward from Damascus and the further east to the sea.

Moreover, Nature around Him had many things to lift His thoughts into another world. The hillsides about Nazareth were wooded, but not with the giant cedars that were common in Lebanon further north ; rather, because of the shallow soil, it was a district of bush and stunted growth. But this made only the more abundant the birds of the air, not one of which would fall to the earth without His Father's will. He had contemplated them all ; the raven, soaring solitary above a mountain-top ; the sparrows twittering beneath the gables ; the multitudinous flock, gathering in a single tree towards evening, and making a stir as if all the winged creatures of the earth had found their home within its branches. All had their wherewithal to live, none was in want ; unlike poor men who earned their bread by the sweat of their brow, these playmates of God lived for the day and were content.

Behold the birds of the air
They sow not
Neither do they reap
Nor gather into barns
And your heavenly Father feedeth them.

Even the hen with her brood in the barnyard had won His affectionate attention ; and beautifully would He one day use it to His purpose. For it was a memory, and not, for once, an illustration before His eyes, that found Him the words for His lament :

Jerusalem, Jerusalem
Thou that killest the prophets

And stonest them that are sent to thee
How often would I have gathered thy children
As the hen doth gather her chickens
Under her wings
And thou wouldest not !

There was growing Nature all around Him which could
not but leave its impress on a village boy, very different
from that of a busy city

The grass of the field
Which is to-day
And to-morrow is cast into the oven
(And yet which) God doth so clothe ;

or again :

The lilies of the field
How they grow
They labour not
Neither do they spin
But I say to you
That not even Solomon in all his glory
Was arrayed as one of these.

There were the vineyards with their vines, stretched along
the built-up ledges on the eastern slope that ran down from
the village, with their cactus hedges around them, their
wine-presses dug into the ground, their watch-towers set
in their midst.   There were the fig-trees running up the
walls of the houses, their broad leaves affording shelter
from the heat of the sun ;   the thistles and thorns among
the rocks, which spread so rapidly when the ground was
neglected.   There were the ditches dug for irrigation, the
wells in the fields for watering the sheep and cattle, into
which, at times, an animal might fall ;   all these became
part of the mind of the growing Boy, and some day would
serve Him well when the time came for Him to teach.
There were the animals.   Nowhere does Jesus mention
horses, for no Nazarene would have owned a horse ;   and
seldom would one have been seen in Nazareth, though in
Jerusalem they would not have been rare.   But there were
the other beasts of burden ;   the ox and the ass, doing their
work, singly or yoked together, in the fields or about the
village ;   or the camel in the distant caravans, the largest

animal the Boy would have seen, so that later He would use it in contrast with the smallest :

> Straining at gnats
> And swallowing camels.

There were the flocks, the snow-white but helpless sheep, running from strangers, quiet when their master was near ; the black-haired goats, grazing alongside on the hills ; at evening all coming home and separating, each knowing its own pen and its own shepherd. And there were the wild beasts ; the silver fox, the terror of the vineyards, which Jesus had seen, as darkness fell, creeping up the hill from its lair in the rock below ; the wolf, the shepherd's terror, coming down from its home in the open country towards Syria ; the pariah dog, the scavenger of the village, the despised of all men ; the snake slipping through the scene, the scorpion under many a stone ; all these Jesus had come to know as every villager knew them, while He grew and waxed strong, developing in wisdom, age, and grace before God and man.

Then there was the weather. He had looked eastward in the morning, across Galilee towards the distant East, and had watched the rising sun don his morning robes of red and gold ; westward to the sea in the evening, and had beheld him go down as it were in a world on fire. He had learnt what these signs meant to the husbandmen about Him, He had heard them discussed at their cottage doors :

> When it is evening you say
> It will be fair weather
> For the sky is red
> And in the morning
> To-day there will be a storm
> For the sky is red and lowering.

He had observed the winds, and the difference they made, the west wind from across the sea bringing its welcome rains, the south wind coming up from Egypt and the Sinai deserts, bringing its scorching dryness.

> And he said to the multitudes
> When you see a cloud coming from the west
> Presently you say
> A shower is coming

And so it happeneth
And when you see the south wind blow
You say, there will be heat
And it cometh to pass.

He had seen the sunshine, and the rain fall, and the crops grow, for all men alike, and had praised His Father in heaven

Who maketh his sun to rise
Upon the good and the bad
And raineth
Upon the just and the unjust.

And as with the weather, so with the changing of the seasons. There had been the early sowing time, immediately after the winter rains or before they were yet over, and the Boy had seen the seed fall, some on the footpath that passed through the field, some on the rocky ground that rose above the earth, some among the thorns and cactus, some on the well-tilled soil. He had watched the wheat grow from day to day :

First the blade
Then the ear
Afterwards the full corn in the ear.

He had looked across the fields ' white for the harvest ', and had seen the farmers gather together and go out to reap :

Immediately he putteth in the sickle
Because the harvest is come.

He had stood by as they brought it home and stored it in their granaries ; He had heard them reckon up its worth, sometimes only moderate, thirtyfold, sixtyfold, sometimes so great, a hundredfold, that the owner had contemplated building yet greater barns. Then had followed the vintage, down the slope that caught all the morning sun, and idle hands had been given occupation, as much as they would. New goatskins had had to be prepared, for the old ones were unsafe for the new wine ; and then there had followed the Feast of Tabernacles, the harvest festival when all had made merry. Year after year Jesus had been through it all ; as one of the villagers He had taken His part ; henceforth His thoughts would often fall back on the familiar setting of the sowing and the reaping, the sheep and their pasturing, the birds of the air and the flowers of the field.

II

Next, how much did Jesus learn from the men and women around Him ! Judged by ordinary standards, the school in which He was trained was no model ; it was not one that would have commended itself to any educational expert. Even the neighbours were wont to say :

> Can anything of good
> Come out of Nazareth ?

while the Nazarenes themselves thought so little of one another that when one of them showed himself in any way superior they ' were scandalised in his regard ', and asked in protest :

> How came this man
> By this learning ?

Nevertheless, it was Nazareth, and Nazareth alone in all the world, which could be given the title bestowed upon it by St. Luke :

> Nazareth
> Where he was brought up.

On that account, we may be sure, Nazareth ever held a special place in the heart of Jesus, and, it would seem, holds a special place there to this day.

Now Nazareth was then, as it is now, altogether out of the way of the busy world. No main high road went through it, though three at least were at some miles distant ; but a single mile in those days, especially if mountains intervened, might effectually cut off all connexion. It was a town of husbandmen, and little or nothing more, insignificant, unknown ; before the time of Our Lord there seems to have been no mention of it anywhere, after His time its name occurs only in connexion with His memory. Its inhabitants, a few thousand at most, were shepherds or farmers, cultivators of the soil, none of them of any great wealth ; only on the outskirts, in the direction of Cana and distant Sephoris, would have been the homes of a few who owned more land than others, and who hired keepers for their sheep, or labourers for their vineyards when the fruit was ripe. In the narrow streets of Nazareth—perhaps we ought even to say, in the one narrow street that ran from south to north up the rocky hillside—Jesus, the Son of the Carpenter, lived among a people to whom time was of little account ; whose day was divided by the sun, who would go out to their fields after dawn, and in the evening, when the day's work was done, would sit on the slabs round the wineshop, or in the market-place, or outside the synagogue at the top of the street, discussing their flocks or their crops, discussing one another, quarrelling at times and, when they did, calling each other foul names. There would be willing workers among them and there would be idlers ; men who would complain of their lot, and men who, with Asiatic patience, would stare before them and say nothing ; those who had their own plot, or even field, to cultivate, and those who would live by hire. All of these, in going His rounds as Joseph's son and errand-boy, Jesus would inevitably come to know. He would be among them, but not of them, for His trade was different from theirs ; in the East the village carpenter, or blacksmith as we might now call him, is a man apart, whose hours of work cannot coincide with those of others, for he is at the beck and call of all. And in their turn the villagers would know Him as the carpenter's apprentice, who mended their carts or their ploughs, the water-pipes or their door-handles, differing in this, and perhaps in this only, from other boys of His age.

But, as we have just said, this alone made Him live His life somewhat apart. While others rested the carpenter must often stay at his work ; while they have their fields and their herds to take them out of the village, he must remain in his shed. He would observe these men go out to their labour in the morning and return at sunset ; He would hear their language as He passed them by, often coarse enough, sometimes violent, and the day would come when He would put what He heard to good purpose.

I say to you
Not to swear at all
Neither by heaven for it is the throne of God
Nor by the earth for it is his footstool
Nor by Jerusalem for it is the city of the great king

> Neither shalt thou swear by thy head
> Because thou canst not make one hair white or black
> But let your speech be yea, yea, no, no
> And that which is over and above these
> Is of evil

Seldom if anywhere in the Gospels do we catch an echo of the country village streets more marked than in this passage.

There were others, too, whom He had noticed ; the rich land-owner, who hired his hands in the market-place and was known to pay fair wages ; another who made much of his possessions, and spurned the beggar at his door. There was the generous possessor of wealth, and there was the miser, who had suspicion lest thieves might break in and steal, who grieved that the moth consumed his locked up clothing, and the rust destroyed his metal tools, who was for ever anxious about the morrow, and found no contentment anywhere. Jesus the youth, passing from door to door in His rounds, had observed all these and pitied them ; and one day He would take just these as the practical matter of His teaching :

> Be not solicitous therefore
> Saying, What shall we eat ?
> Or what shall we drink ?
> Or wherewith shall we be clothed ?
> Be not therefore solicitous for to-morrow
> For the morrow will be solicitous for itself
> Sufficient for the day is the evil thereof.

Do not these last words alone throw light on the life that was lived by Joseph, and Mary and Jesus in their cottage and workshop at the edge of the town ?

There were also women of the village, and of these it is worth noting that one finds in His later descriptions always the same type. We have no ladies of the city, no women of wealth living in luxury ; instead we have the busy housewife sweeping her cottage, anxious about the penny she has lost and, when she finds it, unable to restrain her joy. She must run to her neighbour and tell her all about it, and they must stand together at the door and talk. He has seen her in the early morning, grinding her corn with a companion and singing as she grinds, later in the day kneading her dough as she prepares the

family-meal, in the evening, if her husband has been kept
out late at the sheepfold, setting a candle in the window
to light him home.   He has heard her pleading with her
elders, the rulers of the village, when a court has been
held, for this species of local self-government was
universal ; He has heard her with eastern perseverance
pleading and pleading till at last, merely to be rid of her
they have granted her request. Especially He has noticed
the widows of the little town, for in the East a woman's
lot, without a man to care for her, is very hard ; more
than once in His later life it is emphasised that some
woman to whom He spoke a kind word, or for whom He
did a kind thing, was a widow.

And there were the children.   He who in later life
could say :

> Suffer the children
> And forbid them not to come to me
> For the kingdom of heaven is for such,

had a place in His heart open for children, not then for
the first time. He who later could set up a child as the
model for all men, knew by experience what children
were.   He who could denounce scandal given to a child
with a vehemence and condemnation almost without
parallel, who could promise a reward everlasting to one
who gave so little as a cup of water to a child in need, had
witnessed in His time both the one and the other.   He
who, at the end, could find no fonder way of speaking to
His own than,

> My little children
> I will not leave you orphans
> I will come to you,

had assuredly noticed orphan children and helped them
when He had lived amongst them at Nazareth.   He had
watched children at play on the market square, close by
the synagogue school ; He had heard their little quarrels,
that had brought tears to their eyes. He had seen parents
find bread for them when they had asked for it ; on the
other side He had beheld and loved that simplicity, that
love and trust in the nature of a child which He would one
day make the model for all the children of God.

Last of all there were the members of His own household; cousins and aunts, it would seem, and, most of all, the two with whom he lived. From the first, He had much to learn by what He endured; those of whom it is later said that

Neither did his brethren believe in him,

were not likely to have made Him of much account when He lived with them in their street. But from Joseph, and from Mary, how much did He not learn?

And Jesus himself was beginning
Being as it was supposed
The son of Joseph.

This alone tells us much of the intimacy of the Holy Family: a family that lived very much by itself, of which there was little to know, making no special mark in the village community, doing its ordinary routine work; taken for granted; when later it is asked:

Is not this the son of Joseph?
Is not this the carpenter's son?
His mother, do we not know her?

we may infer how little either the Son, or the mother or foster-father, had been noticed by their fellow-villagers, except that they had done the work that was theirs. We may infer, too, how far the likeness of the foster-father had been stamped upon the foster-son; they were 'of a trade', and the ways of the one would, almost of necessity, have been adopted by the other.

And if that was true of Joseph, still more must it have been true of Mary. The artist is faithful to reality who makes a likeness of features between mother and son; the psychologist is right who sees the qualities, and virtues, and ways of the mother reproduced in her child. For, though it is true that Jesus was always the perfect Man, yet even perfection, in a human being, must be expressed in some special way, must have a personality of its own; and the Boy inherited or learnt by natural imitation, as a child must, His way from His mother, her tone of voice, her manner of speaking, her footsteps, her gesture. He learnt it from her who was the 'blessed among women,' whose 'lowliness' the Lord had regarded, whom later a woman could picture in her mind from the sight of the Son when she cried:

> Blessed is the womb that bore thee
> And the breasts that gave thee suck.

III

In surroundings such as these, under these influences, Jesus ' grew in wisdom, and age, and grace before God and man.' Till His sixth year, according to the custom of His people, He was entirely in His mother's care ; what He learnt from her it is needless, useless, to attempt to describe. At the age of six He would go to the village school, in or beside the synagogue ; every village had its school. There He would learn to read and write—we have instances of His doing both—but probably little more, and the reading was almost confined to the Scripture and its commentaries. At a certain age those who wished to go further left their village for higher schools elsewhere, the highest of them being in Jerusalem.

Here it seems necessary to consider the Jewish mind in regard to learning, for it explains much of the criticism of Jesus by the scribes and doctors which may be easily misunderstood. In the West, caste and class distinctions are created principally by wealth ; in the East it is almost, if not quite entirely, a matter of birth. But among the Jews, in the time of Jesus, it was neither of these ; a man was held to be of no higher status merely because he was rich ; the descendants of the Twelve Tribes of Israel, or of what remained of them, were all equally proud of their origin, they were all ' sons of Abraham.' Instead, from time immemorial, but especially since the Restoration under Esdras, there had grown up a social distinction based upon learning, and especially learning in the Law. The students of the Law, under the various rabbis, were a class apart ; even from so far away as Tarsus, Saul, a Roman citizen, thought it worth his while to come to Jerusalem that he might graduate in this school. At a certain age, about his twelfth year, a Jewish boy chose his path in life, and either continued in that course in which he was born, or deliberately accepted his vocation to that more ascetic

state which was implied in that of a student of the Law.
It was thought impossible that the labourer could also be
a scholar. In illustration of this, there is the striking
passage in the *Book of Ecclesiasticus*, where the Son of
Sirach makes a sharp contrast. Because of its importance
and its bearing on certain scenes in the Gospels, we
venture to quote it in full.

1

The wisdom of the scholar cometh by his time of leisure,
   He whose affairs are few may study.
How could he be learned that holdeth the plough,
   And glorieth in the goad he wieldeth,
That driveth oxen and is occupied in their labours,
   Whose whole talk is of the offspring of bulls ?
He giveth his mind to turn up furrows ;
   And his care is to give the kine fodder.

2

So likewise is engaged every carpenter and builder,
   That laboureth in his craft night and day.
So the engraver that cutteth the seal,
   Designing all manner of exquisite figures.
He giveth his mind to copy the device
   And his care is to finish the picture.

3

Similarly doth the smith standing by the anvil
   Closely watch the iron he shapeth.
The vapour of the fire wasteth his flesh,
   And he fighteth with the heat of the furnace.
The noise of the hammer deafeneth his ears,
   But his eyes are on the pattern beside him.
He giveth his mind to excel in his workmanship,
   And his care is a perfect polish.

4

No less busy is the potter sitting at his work,
   Turning the wheel with his feet.
He fashioneth the clay with his arm,
   His back is bent long ere he is old.

He giveth his mind to fire the glaze,
And his care is to keep clean his kiln.

5

ALL THESE trust in the work of their hands,
   And each is clever in his own craft.
Without them cities cannot be built,
   Where they dwell, none dies of starvation,
But they are not called to the assembly of wise men,
   On the judges' seat they shall not sit.
The ordinance of the law they do not understand,
   They are not found in the counsel of the learned.
Their knowledge is limited to the skill of their hands,
   And their concern to the work of their trade.
QUITE DIFFERENT he whose mind is engaged
   To study and search the law of the Most High.

6

He will seek out the wisdom of the ancients,
   And peruse the writings of prophets.
He will con the sayings of renowned men,
   And enter into the subtleties of parables.
He will find the secrets of grave maxims,
   And be conversant with graceful comparisons.

7

His service shall be sought by the great,
   At the court of princes he shall appear.
He shall travel through far-off countries,
   To study the customs of foreign nations.
His heart resorts early to the Lord that made him,
   In the sight of the Most High he offers his prayers.
He will open his mouth in supplication,
   To ask pardon for failings and sins.

8

If so it should please God, the great Lord,
   He shall be filled with the spirit of wisdom.
He shall pour forth words of understanding,
   And shall acknowledge the gift of the Lord.
He shall direct his counsel and learning
   To meditate on the secrets of God.

9

Forth shineth from him that which he hath learned,
  He glorieth in the knowledge of God's love.
Many shall commend his understanding,
  His wisdom shall never be forgotten.
The memory of him shall not fade away,
  His name shall live for ever and ever.
Nations shall rejoice in his learning,
  And multitudes shall declare his praise.[1]

In the light of this passage, and of what has already been said, the scene in the Temple when Jesus was lost and found becomes full of significance. He was at the age when a Jewish boy made his choice of a vocation. Speaking humanly, with the work of the future before Him, it would have been no strange thing if He had stayed on in Jerusalem, that He might grow yet more in the wisdom of the ancients ; to leave home and parents for this purpose was nothing uncommon, and His mother, when she put her question, would almost certainly have had this in mind.

Why hast thou done so to us ?

i.e. Why didst thou not let us know that thou hadst chosen this vocation ? And yet, He did not ; He had not told them because He had not meant to stay in the schools. Instead, after He had blessed the student's life by thus far partaking in it, He chose to go down with Mary and Joseph, back to Nazareth, where there was no further school, and to be subject to them. He chose to take up that career in life which, on the evidence of the Son of Sirach, and of all the conventions of the day, was inconsistent with growth in wisdom and learning. It was not, therefore, wholly without reason that later His fellow-Nazarenes complained:

How came this man by all these things
And what wisdom is this that is given to him ?

[1] Ecclesiasticus xxxviii, 25–xxxix, 14. The above rendering is that of the 'ate Fr. A. Rembold, S.J., Professor of the Old Testament at Valkenburg.

Is not this the carpenter
The son of Mary ?

And they were scandalised in regard of him.

Still less need we wonder that the same taunt is urged
against Him in the Temple, when He challenged and
refuted the science of the time on its own ground:

How doth this man know letters
Having never learned ?

Nor again need we wonder at the many attempts to
suppress this new Rabbi with contempt:

We are the disciples of Moses
We know that God spoke to Moses
But as to this man
We know not from whence he is.

To all of these Jesus had but one answer. No, it was
true, He had not learnt in any of their schools ; His
teaching was not part of their philosophy. The Child
that had been born in Bethlehem, and not in the palace
of Augustus, was the Boy who would be a carpenter's
apprentice, and not a scholar of the schools, ' that no flesh
might glory ' in the sight of God.

My doctrine is not mine
But his that sent me.

Deliberately, when He came to make His choice, He had
chosen ' to be about His Father's business ', and that was
to go back to His home, to learn His foster-father's trade,
to be ' brought up ' among those from whom the Wise
Man had expressly said that wisdom was not to be expected. Yet He learnt wisdom in another school, that of
real life. If, when He sat, at the age of twelve,

In the midst of the doctors
Hearing them
And asking them questions
All that heard him were astonished
At his wisdom and his answers ;

though through the intervening eighteen years He was
silent, we need not be surprised that later He spoke

> As one having authority
> And not as the scribes ;

that

> Never man spoke
> Like this man ;

that in after years He should be remembered as One who
was

> Mighty in word and work
> Before God and man.

In spite of His upbringing He could bid the propounders
of the Law

> Search the Scriptures
> For these give testimony of me.

He could tell them that if they understood Moses as they
should, they would know Him also ; He could quote the
Scriptures as one to whom they were familiar ; even when
they sought to catch Him by means of difficult interpretations, He could retort the argument and send them away
in such mood that they ' dared ask him no more questions.' Noe, and Abraham, and Lot, Moses and Elias, the
Woman of Sarepta and Naaman the Syrian, Jonas the
Prophet and David the Psalmist-King, all in their turn
came familiarly to His mind when they served His need,
no less than the birds of the air or the lilies of the field.
He would quote with the ease of one to whom they were
well known—not with the subtle word-splitting of the
scribes, but with the insight of one who had weighed them
apart, and had learnt their meaning in the sight of His
Father who had inspired them. Especially we find Him
dwelling on Isaias, the Prophet of the Servant of God,
who spoke more than others of His suffering, His mercy
and compassion, His freedom and triumph ; at the end,
when He dwells on the future, we hear Him speaking in
the language of the Prophet of desires, Daniel.

And yet, for the most part, when He speaks of Himself
it is the impress of the life at Nazareth that most strongly
colours the picture. John the Baptist could call Him the
Lamb of God, the King of whom he himself was the herald,

the Bridegroom in whose presence he could do nothing
but rejoice. Others might say, under the influence of the
learned in the Law, that He was John the Baptist come
back again to life, or Elias, or Jeremias, or one of the
prophets. But when He speaks of Himself, His thoughts
go back to the hillsides round Nazareth, to the life He had
witnessed during the long years of waiting, and He would
find there what He most desired for His purpose:

Amen, Amen I say to you,
I am the door of the sheep
All others as many as have come
Are thieves and robbers
And the sheep heard them not
I am the door
By me if any man enter in
He shall be saved
And he shall go in and go out
And find pastures
The thief cometh
But for to steal and to kill and to destroy
I am come that they may have life
I am the good shepherd
And I know mine
And mine know me.

V

THE WITNESS OF GALILEE

I

THERE is a passage in the synoptic Gospels, common, that is, to St. Matthew, St. Mark, and St. Luke, though it is found in different places, and is used by each in a somewhat different way. St. Matthew gives it at the beginning of his account of the Public Life, before he has told us anything of consequence, as if he would make it a kind of introduction to all that was to follow. He says (iv, 23-25):

> And Jesus went about all Galilee
> Teaching in their synagogues
> And preaching the gospel of the kingdom
> And healing all manner of diseases
> And every infirmity among the people
> And his fame went throughout all Syria
> And they presented to him all sick people
> That were taken with divers diseases and torments
> And such as were possessed of devils
> And lunatics and those that had the palsy
> And he cured them
> And many people followed him
> From Galilee and from Decapolis
> And from Jerusalem and from Judæa
> And from beyond the Jordan.

Obviously, it would seem, coming as it does before a single miracle has been described or a single sermon recorded, when as yet he has only told of Jesus by the Jordan with John the Baptist, in the desert with the Tempter, and by the Lake of Galilee, St. Matthew intended this passage as a sort of general background to all he was about to say; one might perhaps question whether the ' multitudes ' here mentioned, coming from such different places,

are to be taken as belonging to any one time or place. In
St. Mark the description comes much later ; it occurs
immediately before the account of the choosing of the
Twelve. Already in an earlier place he has generalised in
similar terms, but much more briefly (i, 39):

> And he was preaching in their synagogues
> And in all Galilee
> And casting out devils.

Now, after much has been told, so that we are less taken
by surprise, and after we have reached a formal break with
the Pharisees which has seemed to necessitate a new
method of campaign, the Evangelist writes (iii, 7-10):

> But Jesus retired with his disciples to the sea
> And a great multitude followed him
> From Galilee and Judæa
> And from Jerusalem and from Idumæa
> And from beyond the Jordan
> And they about Tyre and Sidon
> A great multitude
> Hearing the things which he did
> Came to him.
> And he spoke to his disciples
> That a small ship should wait on him
> Because of the multitude lest they should throng him
> For he healed many
> So that they pressed upon him to touch him
> As many as had evils.

St. Luke gives a similar summary, not before, but after
the choosing of the Twelve, when, however, like St.
Mark, he had already recorded enough to justify the
generalisation (vi, 17-19):

> And coming down with them
> He stood in a plain place
> And the company of his disciples
> And a very great multitude of people
> From all Judæa and Jerusalem
> And the sea coast both of Tyre and Sidon
> Who were come to hear him
> And to be healed of their diseases

And they that were troubled with unclean spirits
Were cured
And all the multitude sought to touch him
For virtue went out from him
And healed all.

It will be easily seen that, though each evangelist has made use of the description in his own way, and in a different place in his narrative, still, from the use of the same phrases, from the accounts of the multitudes and districts from which they came, from the allusions to the same events and miracles, the source is the same. Either the writers have made use of a common original, or they have adapted the passage from each other ; of the two, since all give the impression that they are writing from memory, the first would seem to be most likely. In either case all clearly recognise it as exactly suited to their purpose ; wherever it may be placed, they look on it as an accurate summary of the early period of Our Lord's public life. In other words, in the first general impression of Our Lord which all three evangelists put before us, one trait at least is unmistakable, so unmistakable that to mention it is almost a platitude. It is, not merely that

He went about doing good,

as it is said in another place, but that, precisely by this means, by the good He did, He drew all kinds of people to Him, from Tyre by the sea in the east, from the land beyond the Jordan in the west, from Syria in the north and from Judæa in the south.

It may be well to follow the echoes of this description in other places. St. Matthew keeps it always before him, and from time to time comes back to it. More than once he repeats almost the same words, as if he would say that this is the best concise account he can give of the Master whom he wishes to describe. Thus, after recording a series of miracles, gathered together from different times and places, he sums up (ix, 35):

Jesus went about all the cities and villages
Teaching in their synagogues
And preaching the gospel of the kingdom
And curing every disease
And every infirmity.

Again, when the disciples of John come to Our Lord, and ask Him for proof of His mission, St. Matthew, followed by St. Luke, seems to linger with delight on the answer:

> Go and relate to John
> What you have heard and seen
> The blind see
> The lame walk
> The lepers are cleansed
> The deaf hear
> The dead rise again
> The poor have the gospel preached to them.

To St. Matthew, always alive to the fulfilment of prophecy, the reply of Jesus was as much as to say that in Him, and in the things He did, were accomplished the saying of the prophet (Is. xxxv, 4-6):

> Say to the faint-hearted
> Take courage and fear not
> Behold your God will bring you
> The reward of recompense
> God himself will come
> And save you.
> Then shall the eyes of the blind be opened
> And the ears of the deaf shall be unstopped
> Then shall the lame man leap as a hart
> And the tongue of the dumb shall be free.

Further, in another place, after the journey of Jesus beyond the boundary of Palestine, before He returns to His work in Capharnaum and Galilee, while He is still in a pagan, or at least a semi-pagan district, we find St. Matthew concluding with the following summary (xv, 30, 31):

> There came to him great multitudes
> Having with them dumb men and blind
> Lame and maimed
> And many others
> And they cast them down at his feet
> And he healed them
> So that the multitudes marvelled
> Seeing the dumb speak
> The lame walk

The blind see
And they glorified the God of Israel.

In these and other like places St. Matthew never tires of reproducing the picture, each time in almost the same terms, on the one hand of Jesus overwhelmed with works of charity, on the other of the multitudes drawn to Him, to glorify and love Him, precisely on their account. St. Mark repeats the same in his own way ; he particularly calls attention to the crowds that thronged about Jesus, so as to make His very life among them a weariness. Early in his Gospel, in the very first chapter, he tells us how the crowds had already grown so great that (i, 45),

He could not go openly into the city
But was without in desert places
And they flocked to him from all sides.

And almost immediately after :

He entered into Capharnaum
After some days
And it was heard that he was in the house
And many came together
So that there was no room
No, not even at the door.

Yet once more, with only one event intervening (ii, 13):

And he went forth again to the sea side
And all the multitude came to him
And he taught them.

Last of all, in the next chapter, as if he would mark a climax of this incessant thronging in the early part of His career (iii, 20, 21):

And they came to a house
And the multitude came together again
So that they could not so much as eat bread
And when his friends heard of it
They went out to lay hold on him
For they said
He is become mad.

In repeated passages such as these, all occurring in the first three chapters of his Gospel, St. Mark, the spokesman of St. Peter, shows to us Jesus wearing Himself out in doing good to all alike, making no exceptions, till the people follow Him in crowds, and take His beneficence for granted. We are not, therefore, surprised when, in another place, Peter felt justified in making the remonstrance (v, 31):

Thou seest the multitude thronging thee
And sayest thou
Who hath touched thee ?

St. Luke adds yet another detail to the picture, at the opposite extreme to that of St. Mark. In the eyes of St. Luke not only does Jesus do good to all alike, and in general ; He performs His labour of love to each one in particular. Thus he says in one place (iv, 40):

When the sun had set
All who had in their houses any sick of any disease
Brought them to him
And he cured them
Laying his hands on each one in turn.

In the same way, in many other places, the physician Luke shows us how Jesus laboured, not for large numbers only, but also for single individuals ; how He gave His attention to each one, with a heart that felt for individual suffering. It is he who tells specially of individual cures. He alone relates the story of the Raising of the Widow's Son to life at Naim, with its attention to tiny details (vii, 13):

Whom when the Lord had seen
Being moved with mercy towards her
He said to her: Weep not.

It is St. Luke who gives us, and that at great length, the account of the conversion and defence of the Woman who was a Sinner (vii, 37) ; he, too, alone records the Parable of the Good Samaritan (x, 30). In the curing of an infirm woman he relates how Jesus specially (xiii, 12, 13):

Called her to him,

and

Laid his hands upon her.

He tells the story of the man sick of the dropsy (xiv, 2) ; the Parable of the Lost Sheep, of the Prodigal Son, of the

Rich Man and Lazarus, are all told by St. Luke, as if he would counteract any impression that Jesus sacrificed the individual for numbers. He points out how, when Jesus cured ten lepers together, nevertheless He counted them; He knew them, each (xvii, 12). He attended to the blind man on the roadside, though His companions would have him passed by (xviii, 35); when the publican Zacheus only wished to get a sight of Him in the crowd, Jesus responded by leaving the multitude alone, and choosing his house for His resting-place that night (xix, 5).

In the story of the passion St. Luke reveals to us how Jesus had a special prayer for Peter (xxii, 31), a special word for Judas (xxii, 48), special sympathy for those who had sympathy for Him on His way to Calvary, for Simon of Cyrene (xxiii, 26) and for the weeping women (xxiii, 27), a special forgiveness for the penitent thief who spoke but a word in His defence.

In the Gospel of St. John this characteristic is emphasised in yet another way. Here we find Him not only, as elsewhere, labouring without respite in good works, but appealing to those same works as proof of His mission from His Father. He who had set before His hearers the Father,

> Who maketh his sun to rise on the good and bad
> And raineth upon the just and the unjust,

could say of Himself (v, 17):

> My Father laboureth until now
> And I also labour;

in another place (ix, 4):

> I must do the works of my Father
> While it is day
> The night cometh
> When no man can work;

and again (x, 25):

> The deeds which I do in the name of my Father
> These give testimony of me.

He will even use this same proof of His works as a challenge to His enemies; and these works are called just 'good works', they are not called miracles, as if it were their goodness, and not the miracles, that was their chief evidence for Him. Thus (x, 32):

Many good works have I shown you
From my Father
For which of those works do you stone me ?

Or again (x, 38):

If you will not believe me
Believe my works
That you may know and believe
That the Father is in me
And I in the Father.

Or, lastly (xiv, 11, 12), even when speaking aside to His own:

Do you not believe that I am in the Father
And the Father in me ?
At least believe
Because of the works that I do.

II

This, then, was a first general impression produced upon others by Our Lord Jesus Christ in real life, during the first months of His apostolate in Galilee, and preserved unchanged afterwards, no matter what were the vicissitudes through which He passed. He was of unsparing labour ; He gave of His best to all alike, good and bad, Jew and Gentile. While giving to all, He showed a personal interest in each ; He made an appeal to the things He did as something that distinguished Him, indeed, as proof of His identity. All four evangelists, but especially the first three, put this aspect of Him before us from the very beginning, almost before they have given us evidence in detail, as if they would have us bear it always in mind, whatever else they may say. For indeed it was something new. In all the Old Testament there is not a single character whose life would be summed up in the single sentence, as the life of Jesus was summed up: 'He went about doing good'. And if none in the Old Testament then certainly none in the pagan world ; however strange it may seem to us, after nineteen centuries of Christianity,

' He went about doing good,' in the time of the evangelists, was a new and strange standard of life, so new, so
strange, that it needed the Son of God to prove it.

When next we come to His teaching, to the practical
advice He gave to those who would be His followers, we
find Him constantly recurring to the one same theme:
' Do good.' With Jesus, if we look at His words carefully,
it is not so much a question of being good, of acquiring
virtues, of excelling in prayer or mortification and the
like. He speaks more of their manifestation and their
fruits, on the one hand of endurance in one form or
another, of ' doing good ' on the other. Always He is
eminently realistic, He seeks for deeds more than for
abstractions ; the word humility is not once to be found
in His mouth, but the act of humility never fails to win
Him. Thus, in the Sermon on the Mount, He places a
summit of perfection, a likeness to God the Father
Himself, in this :

> Do good to those who hate you
> And persecute you
> That you may be the sons of your Father
> Who is in heaven.

Similarly, when He sends out His disciples for the first
time to preach the kingdom, they must preach it as He
preached it, by action more than by word, by ' doing
good ' more than by teaching, and for this He gives them
even His own powers.

> Heal the sick
> Raise the dead
> Cure the lepers
> Cast out devils
> Freely have you received
> Freely give.

When later He pronounces ' Woe ' upon the scribes and
Pharisees, it is not because they are wanting in prayer, not
even because they lack any special virtue ; it is because
they ' say and do not ' ; because they

> Bind heavy and insupportable burdens
> And lay them on men's shoulders.

But with a finger of their own they will not lift them ; because they

> Devour the houses of widows
> Praying long prayers ;

because they

> Tithe mint and anise and cummin
> And have left the weightier things of the law
> Judgement and mercy and faith.

When men ask Him for an example of true life He responds by the story of the Good Samaritan. When one seeks for perfection He replies, looking on the man and loving him:

> If thou wouldst be perfect
> Go sell all that thou hast
> And give to the poor
> And thou shalt have treasure in heaven.

When He promises His reward:

> Come ye blessed of my Father
> Possess the kingdom prepared for you,

it is because

> I was hungry
> And you gave me to eat
> I was thirsty
> And you gave me to drink
> I was a stranger
> And you took me in ;

and if some shall wonder when they did such a thing He will tell them:

> Amen I say to you
> As long as you did it to one of these
> My least brethren
> You did it to me.

There is nothing approaching this in the Old Testament, nothing in any ancient literature, however otherwise noble and inspiring. It would be an almost endless task to follow out this study, and see how this entirely new thing, in the example and teaching of Jesus, impressed

itself by degrees on those who best knew and loved Him.
At one time Peter had said:

We have left all
And followed thee,

and for the moment it was perfection enough, meeting a
noble reward. But soon he was to learn that there was
something more ; that not surrender only, but service
also, was to be the mark of a true disciple:

I have given you an example
That as I have done to you
So you do also
If then I being your Lord and Master
Have washed your feet
You also ought to wash one another's feet
In this shall men know that you are my disciples
If you have love one for another.

And well did Peter learn the lesson. We see him later
in the Temple, beginning to preach where his Master
began:
Silver and gold I have none
But what I have I give thee ;

and later still in his Epistle, when he knows that soon
he must leave his children to the unknown future, he
sums up all his practical doctrine in the words:

But before all things
Have a constant mutual charity among yourselves
For charity covereth a multitude of sins.

Thus was the lesson learnt by the early Church, and
became the first mark of the Christian community, dis-
tinguishing it sharply, and even strangely, from everything else around it. ' See how these Christians love one
another ', was a common description of them all ; and
indeed it was passing strange to see a Philemon take back
a runaway slave, and treat him, no longer as a slave, but
as a son. The Acts of the Apostles are full of the same:

And the multitude of believers
Had but one heart and one soul

Neither did anyone say
That aught of the things that he possessed
Was his own
But all things were common unto them.
For neither was there anyone needy among them
For as many as were owners of lands or houses
Sold them
And brought the price of the things they sold
And laid it down before the feet of the apostles
And distribution was made to every one
According as he had need.

When we read summaries such as these we may well wonder whether they do not contain some exaggeration. Yet the fact is told without any sign of emotion, and the tragic story of Ananias and Sapphira shows how literally the teaching was understood. Similarly, again and again, St. Paul in his Epistles comes back to the same, bidding his disciples 'put on the Lord Jesus Christ', and with Him spend themselves in doing good to others. To quote one passage out of many, after he has written to his beloved, and, it would seem, most mystic-minded Colossians, of the Mystical Body of Christ, he gave as proof of the life of that Body, not prayer, not vision of the supernatural, not even the attainment of high virtue, but, like his Master, the simple practice of charity:

Put ye on therefore
As the chosen of God
Holy and beloved
The heart of mercy
Benignity humility modesty patience
Supporting one another
Forgiving one another
If anyone has a complaint against another.

So it is with the other inspired writers, with St. John, whose 'little children, love one another', has become a Christian password: with St. James, the apostle above all of good works. Does he not sum up the whole of Christian teaching in the words:

Religion pure and undefiled
With God and the Father
To visit orphans and widows in their tribulations
And to keep oneself unspotted from the world?

And he concludes his rugged Epistle with the last recommendation:

My brethren
If anyone of you shall have wandered from the truth
And someone converts him
He should know
That whosoever shall cause a sinner to be converted
From the error of his ways
Shall save his own soul from death
And shall cover a multitude of sins.

To sum up what has been said. This is the witness of the ministry of Christ in Galilee, during His years of success; the general impression remained to the end though the situation altered. It was something new, even startling; so startling as to be revolutionary, creating a new ideal and outlook on human life. And fidelity to that ideal is our Christianity; in practice, at least, and in its external manifestation, as Jesus Christ Our Lord, by word and example, has taught it to us. By this He first struck those whom He drew to Himself, by the same He would have His Mystical Body be conspicuous in the world in which it lives. When we are most proud of our faith, when we are most conscious that 'we live, now not we, but Christ lives in us', then we respond most to this appeal, and long in ourselves to go and do likewise: 'the charity of Christ driveth us.' That we, as children of the Church of Jesus Christ, as living members of His living body, as fingers of that hand which gave to each and all, should be marked by our service of the poor; that the sick and feeble should be nursed by no more tender hands than ours; that the lowest outcast should know that by us at least he is not ignored; that none should be excluded from our love, from our desire for their good, and to give to them, if so we may, the best thing we possess, the knowledge of the truth which is ours; that we should not be content with merely giving of our substance, but also of ourselves, our time, our interest, our labour; this is to 'put on the Lord Jesus Christ', to live the life He lived; this is the spirit of Him who 'went about doing good', who 'did all things well', who was 'mighty in word and work before God and all the people', who 'loved me and gave Himself for me'. Is it too much to say that the revelation of Christ, in practice, is the dominion of fraternal charity ?

III

And yet if we were to stop here the general impression witnessed to by St. Matthew and the other evangelists would be incomplete. In another place in St. Matthew's Gospel there is a further summary which, to complete the picture, must be put alongside of that we have already considered. After an account of a conflict between Jesus and the Pharisees in Capharnaum the apostle writes (xii, 14-20):

And the Pharisees going out
Made a consultation against him
How they might destroy him
But Jesus knowing it
Retired from thence
And many followed him
And he healed them
And he charged them
That they should not make him known
That it might be fulfilled
Which was spoken by Isaias the prophet saying
Behold my servant
Whom I have chosen
My beloved
In whom my soul hath been well pleased
I will put my spirit upon him
And he shall show judgement to the Gentiles
He shall not contend nor cry out
Neither shall any man hear his voice
In the streets
The bruised reed he shall not break
And smoking flax he shall not extinguish
Till he send forth judgement unto victory.

Though the passage occurs in the twelfth chapter of the Gospel, still it is attached to a scene which, in the order of time, when we compare it with its place in the other Gospels, would seem to have occurred much before ; at the close, that is, of what may be called the period of success. At the end of the fourth chapter, when the account of the public life of Jesus has just begun, the

evangelist has introduced it by the first generalisation ;
now, when the Sermon on the Mount has been written
out at length, when representative miracles have been
collected together and described, when the Twelve have
been sent on their first mission, when the opposition has
definitely decided on taking the life of Jesus, the inspired
writer seems again to pause. He looks back on the way
his first generalisation has been illustrated ; he now looks
forward and knows that a change is about to take place.
There is need to add one further touch to the picture he
has drawn. He quotes the prophet Isaias, and sees in
Jesus the fulfilment of that prophecy. But he does both
in his own way, with that free, and almost allegorical,
adaptation which is less comprehensible to us, but was
familiar to the Jews of that time. It may be well to
compare the quotation of St. Matthew with the original.
Isaias (xlii, 1-4) had thus described the Servant of
Jahweh :

Behold my servant, whom I uphold,
My elect, in whom my soul is well pleased
I have put my spirit upon him ;
He shall distribute justice among the nations.
He shall not cry out, he shall not speak aloud,
His voice shall not be heard in the streets,
The bruised reed he shall not break,
And smoking flax he shall not extinguish.
He shall utter justice in truth ;
He shall not be sad or discouraged,
Till he shall have established justice on the earth,
And the islands shall wait for his law.

Thus it is seen that, while the prophet describes the
Servant of Jahweh in His triumph over the world, St.
Matthew used the same description for the moment of
His seeming defeat. Isaias speaks of gentleness and peace-
fulness when He has spread His power to ' the islands ' ;
the evangelist speaks of the same as He retires before the
storm. The hour for battle and victory was not yet, but
the Lord was the same in either case ; He would win, not
as others win, by violence, but by meekness and defeat.
He would not provoke His enemies ; He would not have
His miracles flaunted before their eyes ; He would avoid,
for the present, all controversy with those whose minds
were made up ; there should be no ostentation or dis-

turbance in the public streets on His behalf; Son of God though He was, for the present, till the moment for the further revelation came, He would be known as the Servant; the Servant in whom the Father was well pleased, who had

Emptied himself
Taking the form of a servant
Being made in the likeness of men
And in habit found as man.

He had come to save and not to destroy, that the sinner might live and not perish. In the very same chapter from which the passage we are considering is taken occurs the unforgettable appeal:

Come to me
All you that labour and are burdened
And I will refresh you;

and it follows words describing the claims of Jesus which are worthy of St. John. The Servant of men, the Saviour of men; whatever His enemies might stir up against Him, this characteristic should abide, and should be the foundation of all else. In the strength of that foundation the time would come when He would spread His justice, His rule, to 'the islands', to the nations far away, to the whole earth. ' Blessed are the meek, for they shall inherit the earth.' It was a new concept of the life of service which He had already taught. Let the enemy rage against Him and meditate vain things; the kingdom of service would be spread none the less, and its weapon would be meekness and peace. It is not without significance that the Gospel of meekness and service should abruptly end with the assurance:

All power is given to me
In heaven and in earth
Going therefore teach ye all nations.

This would seem to be the purpose of the prophecy, as it is quoted here. But at the beginning of the passage there is a phrase which throws, and is clearly intended to throw, a flood of light on the mind of Christ:

Jesus knowing it.

The phrase does not occur here alone. From time to time throughout the Gospel story we are reminded, first by one evangelist and then by another, that ' He knew ' ; as if they would have us never forget the unceasing forbearance, while never ceasing to ' do good ', which this abiding knowledge implied. Jesus from the first ' knew what was in man ' (John ii, 24), and it prevented Him from trusting man wholly, from giving to him all He gladly would. He knew, on the other hand, what was in Himself, the perfection of manhood, the fulness of the divinity, the life that was the light of men, shining in the darkness ; and the knowledge that men would have His gifts, but would not have Himself, was the one abiding wound of His life. He knew what was sin better than any man could know it ; its blindness, its folly, its madness, its degradation ; its death-dealing poison, its malice, its defiance of the Father ; its causes and its effects, the one corrupting evil of the human race. All this He knew and felt as He walked through the contaminated valley of this death, and was ' pressed upon ' by those to whom this loathsome foulness was a pastime. Yet He did not condemn, He did not contend nor cry out, He still continued to ' go about doing good ' He longed only to fulfil the promise contained in the name He bore ; but since men would not let Him save them from themselves, at least He would continue to ' do good ' He knew, on the other side, His own supreme sinlessness, so supreme that, unlike any other man that has lived, He could claim it as His prerogative (John viii, 46). All the more, then, when sin surged all about Him, and made light of Him, and treated Him as no better than itself, nay rather worse :

> Now we know
> Thou hast a devil

> He casteth out devils
> By Beelzebub the prince of devils ;

the sense of nausea rose up within Him, so that at times He was indignant (Mark iii, 5), and His heart was torn. Yes, all this, St. Matthew seems to say, yet none the less ' the bruised reed He would not break, and smoking flax He would not extinguish ' ; He would merely be content to ' retire from thence ' for a time.

Jesus knew all, and His knowledge must be taken into

account if we are to measure the breadth of His patience, the depth of His charity, the infinity of His desire. As we have seen, He knew Himself ; on the other hand He knew the worth of these men who conspired against Him. He knew the past, and He knew the future ; both alike, as from time to time He gave proof, lived with Him in an ever-abiding present. He had begun in privation, and ignominy, and suffering ; He looked back on it all and was content. He could look forward into the future and He knew that the same were to be a part, and an essential part, of the lot pre-ordained for Him in this world, the lot He had deliberately chosen for Himself. More that was yet to come had been foretold of Him from the beginning, and though His mother ' understood not ', He had not misunderstood. He had been ' set for the resurrection and the fall of many ' (Luke ii, 34) ; by failure and contradiction, and only so, was He to open a way into the hearts of men. He had accepted it all ; during these thirty years He had endured it in silence. The poverty, the weakness, the labour, were of little account ; the cramping limitation, the sense of exile from His true home, the inaction, were more, and He had borne it all, and already by experience of men He had grown ' in wisdom, and age, and grace before God and men '. And then, in this determined way of self-surrender, deliberate, knowing clearly beforehand all that would be, sparing Himself in no single detail, He had begun His life among men ; since that beginning men had seen to it that His programme should be carried out to the letter. Already in these few months He had been made to feel it ; even in these few months which are often called the period of His success. He had come back to Nazareth, ' where He had been brought up '—the evangelist seems to dwell on the words—and had been thrust out by His own as nothing of worth, nay, fit only to be cast headlong from the hill (Luke iv, 16-30). He had gone up to Jerusalem, to His Father's house, and there, because He had ' gone about doing good ', He had been brow-beaten by the leaders of Jewry, as an upstart, a breaker of the Law, a blasphemer (John v, 1-47). Now, here in Capharnaum, which He had made ' His own city ', and where He had ' gone about doing good ' as nowhere else, forces were gathering against Him ' from all Galilee and from all Judæa ' (Luke v, 17), in the name of Church and State alike, for there were votaries of Herod conspiring with the priests, again to drive Him out, a wanderer once more upon the face of the earth, as if He were another Cain (Genesis iv, 12).

And all this at the outset, before yet He had been able clearly to say either who He was or what was His mission, before He had proclaimed His new Law, of love and forgiveness and 'doing good', superseding that of mere justice, before He had done more than open both His hands, that men might take from Him freely whatever He had to give. In estimating the life and character of Jesus there is no mistake greater than to suppose that at any time, even for a brief interval, He was wholly successful, or that opposition and injustice rose up against Him only as the months passed by. Enmity eyed Him with suspicion by the Jordan in Judæa, before John the Baptist was taken, when as yet He Himself had spoken barely a word (John iv, 1). It faced Him on the Temple steps, the first time He stood there as the Messias (John ii, 18); never once did He mount those steps without a protest, not even at the end on the triumphant day of Palms (Luke xix, 39). It pursued Him everywhere, from first to last, insinuating, questioning, contradicting, attributing false motives, misinterpreting, threatening, plotting; so that at one time He would cry out in disappointment, at another He would protest, at another He in His turn would threaten, at another He would appeal to their common sense of justice, of shame, even to their own religious creed. And when these availed nothing, then for a time He would hide in some distant place, or go into the desert, or retire to some upland town like Ephraim; nowhere for long together could the Son of man find where to lay His head (Matthew viii, 20).

Such was the lot which had befallen Him, even in the early days. He had gone into it with full knowledge that so it would be; and in quoting the prophecy of Isaias in this place the Evangelist seemed desirous to let us know the effect it had upon Him. In spite of it all His arm had not drawn back. Never once had He retaliated; never had the power He had shown He possessed been used by Him to the injury of His worst enemy, or to the most unjust prevaricator's undoing. Before their carping criticisms He had unflinchingly maintained the truth; He had answered every question as it had deserved to be answered, He had spoken plainly of the gross indignity done to Him ; but never once had He retaliated on any individual. He had never treated them as they deserved, still less had He closed His hand and ceased to give. He had seen their blindness and had pitied it, finding in it a reason to excuse rather than a cause for indignation. He had beheld their suffering, in body and in soul, and ignoring His own had relieved it ; though He Himself might not have ' time to take food ', yet they should not go away hungry ; though He was Himself a wanderer, yet

> He had compassion on them
> Because they were distressed
> And lying like sheep that had no shepherd.

Through it all He had uttered no cry of anger, He had stirred up no rival demonstration ; not a bruised reed had He broken ; smoking flax, with any sign of life in it, He had not extinguished. On the contrary, as the rest of His life and His teaching were still more to emphasise, He had entered into the lives of these very men, He had made their sufferings His own. Indeed, in another place, in this very fact St. Matthew sees the fulfilment of another prophecy, another sign by which He might be known, which again, as before, is unexpected.

> And when evening was come
> They brought to him many that were possessed with devils
> And he cast out the spirits with his word
> And all that were sick he healed
> That it might be fulfilled
> Which was spoken by the prophet Isaias saying
> He took our infirmities
> And bore our diseases.

The time would come when this prophecy would be yet more completely fulfilled, and on a far wider plane, but for the moment the Evangelist is content to apply it to this. We can see Levi the publican growing in this appreciation, of One who had called even him to be one of His disciples, and who had never repented of His choice. Levi knew, as few if any of his fellow-apostles knew, what the rough, sordid world contained, and therefore what sojourn in it meant to one like Jesus Christ his Lord. Yet He had endured it all, and it had not altered Him. Not all the uncouth ways of those who had thoughtlessly pressed upon Him, jostled Him in the streets, giving Him not so much as time to eat, who had thronged Him by the water-side so that there was danger, professing by all this their superficial loyalty, but also their lack of understanding ; not all the obstinacy of the Jewish mind, which knew well enough where the truth was to be found, but refused to look for it there ; not all the false interpretations put upon His words, His actions, His motives, His very self, the predetermined prejudice blinding them to every contrary proof ; not all the murmurings against Him, all the evil yet specious contradictions of everything He taught, all the twisting of His words, all the snares and devices carefully prepared to catch Him ; not all the ingratitude, and ignoring, and contempt, and scorn, and gross familiarities to which He was compelled to submit as the feature of His everyday life ; not the malice which knew it was wrong and He right, and hated Him the more on that account ; not all the sin that stalked about before His eyes, flagrant, unashamed, defiant, drowning in jeering laughter its own misery ; none of all this, however it stung His sensitive nature to the quick, was able to quench in Him one spark of that deep compassion which, when it saw the hearts of others bleed, made His own heart bleed in union.

VI

THE WITNESS OF THE TWELVE

WE have seen already how much the evangelists insist on the knowledge Jesus possessed of all that was going on about Him. He was not deceived, says St. John:

> For that he knew all men
> And because he needed not
> That any should give testimony of man
> For he knew what was in man.

He knew always what men would do with Him, and He allowed them to do it:

> He knew from the beginning
> Who they were that did not believe
> And who he was that would betray him ;

nevertheless, while He would let men treat Him as they would, He Himself would go on with His own great work and would accomplish His course. Out of all the turmoil He would draw that stream, a little stream at first, which would grow until one day it would inundate the world. To the eyes of men His life might seem a wandering in a barren wilderness ; He knew that He was leading His own into the Promised Land.

I. THE MANIFESTATION

He would begin from the very beginning, a little child at a mother's breast, with nothing that man could count to His credit. For close on thirty years, in the commonest of common village hamlets, His life would be so common that not one of those about Him would see in Him more than they saw in one another ; when at length He did appear, it would be as a sinner among sinners, nothing else. His first years before the world would be, for the most part, one of comparative inaction, waiting at the gate of

His beloved Judæa, waiting by the Jordan crossing, waiting to be discovered. He would have men find Him for themselves, without any demonstration of His own; He would have them come to Him of their own accord, drawn, first, by the teaching of His herald, John, and then by their own experience. He would have them see for themselves, without any miracles or wonders to awe them, realise from the first His personality, in itself and apart from all else. He would have them captivated by it alone, rise to admiration of it for its own sake, love it, trust in it, cling to it, dream of great conquests because of it, whatever further revelations might come after.

This is what St. John would have us understand when, before Jesus had yet taught anything, he tells us that 'the disciples saw and believed'. Next, He would have them be won by His teaching; by what He said and by the way He said it, authoritative, definite, evident even as He spoke it, without need of any further argument. He would tell them, and as He uttered the words they would know them to be true, of the grandeur of the Kingdom that was theirs; of the oneness of them all, even with Himself, under the roof of a common Father; of the ideal of life in this Kingdom, in this universal family; lastly of Himself, the fulfilment of all Israel's dreams and desires, the longed-for Messias whom the prophets had foretold, the Christ anointed from all ages, the Prophet that was to come, greater than Moses, the King of Israel, the Son of David, the Son of Man, the Son of God. And all this, the compelling sincerity of the Baptist, the witness of His own transparent self, the teaching too sublime not to be true, He would later sanction by His wonder-working power, a confirmation and reward to those who already believed, a sufficient sign to others who hesitated and held back, to His enemies a refutation that could not be denied or gainsaid; but last, and often, for no seeming purpose whatsoever but pure love of human nature, a spontaneous overflowing of His divine affection, as if it would not be restrained.

But throughout, miracles or not, from beginning to end His first appeal would always be for the acceptance of Himself as He was, in Himself and for Himself alone. He would be the Son of Man, *the* Man, the more than man, manifestly, to those that saw, above all other men, in His transparent truth, His sinlessness, His strength,

His inner, fascinating beauty, in His flawless yet simple perfection. Gradually, before those who had eyes to see, He would have the truth that was Himself unfold itself, as the bud unfolds its petals, till at the end He should be recognised for what He was, and accepted, and believed, and trusted utterly, till He should be beloved, and followed, and adored. The personal appeal, that men should come to Him, and acknowledge Him, would always be uppermost in all His teaching, the rest would be chiefly to encourage men to it; with the exception of the embassy from John, as John lay a prisoner in the hands of Herod, only before His enemies does He appeal to His works. To them He says:

> If you will not believe me
> Believe my works;

but to His friends, and to those who were of better will, He lifts them above the evidence of works to higher things:

> Unless you see signs and wonders
> You will not believe.

Even in the Passion, when He is challenged to defend His claim, He says nothing of these signs and wonders; He speaks only of His abiding presence in the people's midst, of their knowledge of Him, of His teaching, of His followers.

Such was His attitude before all men; but with His own, with those twelve whom He ' had chosen Himself that they might be with Him ', those on whom it was His will to place all His plan for the future, His constant argument, as if it were the summary and content of all else, would be overwhelming love. He would give it to them, poured out in extravagant abundance, unashamed, sincere, untrammelled; in the tenderest of welcomes when they made advances to Him: ' Come and see '; in the gentlest, most playful of encouragements when they hesitated; in the easy companionship He would give them, which once given would never be taken back; in the conviction, the certainty beyond all verbal argument, with which His very presence would inspire them. He would take them apart and would teach them, lifting them to heights beyond their hungriest dreams; He would invite them and draw them after Him, with His irresistible, infallible assurance. He would take them one by one and listen to them, He would confer on them His own powers. Meekly He would come down to their level, living with them in their own homes, dining at their board, lying beside them on their matting to sleep. He would protect them, as He would not protect Himself, from abuse, and contempt, from criticism and condemnation ; solemnly, with all the world as witness, He would choose them and set them apart, ' that they might be with him '. Carefully, in word and deed, He would give them an example ; publicly He would declare His preference for them, cherished in His heart as His mother, His brothers and His sisters. He would give them instructions more than He would give to others ; He would work special miracles for them alone, compelling from them more and more belief, inspiring in them ever more trust, proving to them beyond doubt His utter, reliable fidelity and worth. To win their confidence He showed His own confidence in them, whole-hearted and unconditional ; giving to them His own commission and powers, the commission to preach, the powers to work His own miracles. Considerately He would care for them ; ' Come apart with me and rest awhile ' ; thoughtfully He would substitute them for Himself ; zealously, when they were in danger, He would save them from their own folly ; with longing He would appeal for at least their fidelity, when others turned away and walked with Him no more. And all this time He would endure them ; their uncouthness, their forwardness, their thoughtless, familiar ways, their rude interruptions, their signs of self-esteem, their intolerance of others, even their contradiction of Himself. In spite of all they did He would bear with them ; He would warn them, would prepare them for coming evil days, even though they would not understand. Specially He would pray for them, for all in general and for each one in particular ; with constant craving, long-enduring, never flagging, that one day, with the help of the Father in heaven, they might discover who in truth He was and own Him.

Such had been His design in the training of His Twelve, as seen step by step in the Gospel narrative ; there came a day when one understood, and the heart of Jesus overflowed upon him. When at length that day came, the whole attitude of Jesus changed. There followed the loving, and patient, and watchful care with which He further built them up to perfect being and to perfect life ; to prayer and fasting, to recognition and acceptance of the cross, to confidence in poverty, to simplicity and truth like that of a little child, to freedom from all narrowness, to avoidance of all offence, to patience in judgement, to forgiveness and again to forgiveness, to endurance of abuse, to the life of prayer as well as its practice, to the noble and loving fear of God, to careful watchfulness, to the worthy love of others, to the right discernment of real good in men and real evil, to faith, to humility, to the just estimate of wealth, to the proper use of talents, to the glory of sacrifice that comes of love. When we bring the lessons together, and see how step by step He taught them, we realise how carefully, and perseveringly, He gave Himself to the training of the Twelve.

Last of all, when the doom is now imminent, and the clouds are gathering thick and black around Him, for the sake of these Twelve He rides into the city, triumphant in their company and making them share in His triumph. By a living parable He foretells to them what will come, before their eyes He confounds His enemies, showing them His preference for the widow and her mite. When all is over He still takes these beloved Twelve aside and gives them warnings of the future ; He assures them of His special care ; at the general upheaval they shall be protected. What more could He do for them that He has not done ? They listen to what He says, they see what He has done, and they know beyond a doubt ; no matter what may happen in future they can never question it. The impress is stamped on their hearts and can never be effaced ; no, not even Judas can get rid of it. When later they recall those terrible days of separation and suffering it is the first memory that recurs:

> Having loved his own that were in the world
> He loved them unto the end.

II.   THE DISCOVERY

In ways like these Jesus had drawn them to Him through the years, truly with the cords of Adam. And upon men so keen to learn, so enthusiastic, already touched by the Baptist's eloquence and example, so observant, so expectant, so willing to be led, yet withal so raw, so simple and untrained, how would the realisation of this person of Jesus Christ grow ? At first they are shown a mere Galilæan, like to, perhaps inferior to, one of themselves. He is not even from Judæa, as is John the Baptist their leader, but is a working man from Nazareth, whose inhabitants counted for nothing, and from which nothing of good came. He has been in their company already, when He stood to be baptised like the rest, and they have not noticed Him ; when He is first pointed out to them, He makes no impression whatever. Their attention must be called to Him a second time ; again they are induced by John to look at Him. Out of curiosity, more, it would seem, than from any other motive, they follow Him where He walks ; there are no miracles, there is nothing they can mention out of the common way of things, yet at once after the first meeting they come away saying:

We have found the Messias.

A simple glance, a kindly invitation, an unmistakable sincerity makes another describe Him with enthusiasm:

We have found Him
Of whom Moses in the law
And the prophets did write
Jesus
The son of Joseph of Nazareth.

Jesus Bar-Joseph ! Not Jesus the Son of Mary ; they can as yet give Him only the name by which He is known among His fellow-Nazarenes ; they know nothing more. A prophetic word, a reading of character, calls from a third a yet further confession:

Rabbi
Thou art the Son of God
Thou art the King of Israel ;

and thus the process of training begins. Attracted, they can scarcely say why, sanguine, with little tangible ground for their confidence, knowing they are right, though unable to give a word of reason for their choice, these men elect to go with Him. He leads them into Galilee ; at Cana, unexpectedly at a marriage feast, by a miracle they are confirmed in their belief, though what they believed, and why a miracle confirmed it, it would have been hard for them to say. Only this: that the Jesus they followed was true, and therefore the miracle was true, and therefore they were true to themselves in their devotion to Him. He returns to Jerusalem, and acts as its Lord from the first. These fishermen of Galilee are awed by this unknown Nazarene's assumption of authority, alone, without a guard, Jewish or Roman ; His command of the very Temple, His defiance of its rulers in their own domain, His teaching of a Pharisee as if he were a very child ; so that with His inspiration, under His direction, they, too, begin to preach the kingdom and baptise, where John had done at the Jordan crossing. He moves again and they follow ; He is weary with His journey, and He must be the first to be relieved ; He holds converse with an outcast woman, one with whom no self-respecting Jew would deign to speak. They are astonished, but they are not scandalised ; already they have learnt to trust Him too much for that. On the contrary, because He stays in that neighbourhood, among heretic Samaritans, they, too, will stay ; because He mingles with the people, they, too, will share in the work. It is the first step to that universal concept which later is to make them truly Catholic.

A very little later, in the early spring season, when they have perforce gone back to their homes and have taken up their old occupations, He comes to them once more by their cottages on the shore. He invites them to come away after Him ; without a moment's hesitation they leave all and follow ; the fascination of the meeting has grown in the interval to a great desire, and there can be no question of doubt. For the next few months, once they are gathered about Him, the authority, the power, the personal supremacy of the Man that has won their hearts grows upon them. His sure, clear-sighted independence that never hesitates, His certainty of vision, of aim ; His simple yet radical teaching, His deliberate claim against those who would question His right or contradict Him ; His lavish miracles, recognised now for what they were, and, when it so pleased Him, flowing from Him like sunlight from the sun, His forgiveness of sins, His overlordship of the sabbath, His conquest of the multitudes, whensoever they might come, of whomsoever they might be composed—by such revelations of dignity, love, generosity they are won more and more to reverence, devotion, service. On a sudden, one morning, a climax is reached. They have come thus far in knowledge and devotedness ; He must now take them into a yet more intimate circle. After a night of prayer He descends to the multitude ; from all the rest He calls these Twelve apart :

Whom he would himself
That they might be with him
And that he might send them to teach
And cast out devils.

And yet all this time, in spite of the personality that compelled reverence, the superhuman wonders, the authority that set Him above both friend and enemy, there has grown up among them, naturally, unconsciously, a lessening of awe, an increasing familiarity. This Messias, this Son of God, this King of Israel, is nevertheless only Jesus, the carpenter of Nazareth, whose mother they knew, whose brethren are with them, who must needs eat and rest like themselves, who will lie down with them on their cottage floor to sleep. When He must leave one town for another He will almost offer His apologies ; when they make merry He will sit at table with them, and they enjoy the feast unafraid. Men ignore Him and He does not seem to mind ; countrymen condemn Him, as being no more than themselves, bring up His origin against Him, and He does not resent it. Lepers approach Him, who slink away from other men, and from whom other men turn aside ; He is molested where He lives by thoughtless throngs, who invade even His house, and He does not complain. His friends are chosen as He wills, without any regard to convention ; men may find fault with His ways, with His behaviour, with the company He keeps, and He pays no regard to what they say. Whenever He is with His Twelve He is just one of them ; one with them in life and in their manner of living. Do what they will, revere Him as they may and must, still they cannot but find in Him an equal, they cannot but regard Him as one of their own kin.

These two, on the one hand limitless authority, with the nobility of soul that underlies it, on the other meek familiarity, with its self-ignoring lowliness, now become the features stamped upon the minds of these captivated men ; He is at once the absolute Master and the Servant, the Lord and the subject of all. The first He emphasises, so that they may not disregard it, by the thundering significance of the words He now begins to use: ' I say to you ' ; by the royal reward He bestows on one who believes, though he be a mere Gentile ; by more than imperial command of death itself. At the same time, often in the same event, He reveals the second, the kinship of His heart with the hearts of his fellow-men, by His sympathy for a widow woman, His shielding of a woman disgraced, His permitting women to come after Him whose only desire is to follow and serve. Then comes a new phase, another demonstration of His essential oneness with men. For God-man as He is, Lord and Master as they now begin to call Him, nevertheless it is now that He first betrays to His own the wounds that hurt Him ; His dejection because of opposition, His sadness because of failure, even while He clings to them the more, appeals to them the more, calls them His own brethren, works further miracles for them, as if He would bind them the more to Himself. Before their eyes He reveals, in utter simplicity, alike His human strength and His human weakness ; they see Him torn both ways, now with deep affection, now with the sting of abuse, now with pitying compassion, now with hungry longing ; at one time His eyes flash with indignation—' looking upon them with anger '—at another they are wet with tears. When He deals with His own He seems almost to transcend the bounds of human prudence. Before they have yet been trained or tested He trusts them beyond belief ; He sends them forth to preach His doctrine, and to do the work that He had done, multiplying Himself in even such as these unlettered men.

In this way they are won. Familiarity, likeness, has made them one with Him, authority, trust, has lifted them beyond themselves ; these fishermen from the lake of Galilee have courage now for anything. Children as they are, they can now obey Him gladly, though His commands seem beyond all reason. They can believe whatever He may say, though what He says appears utterly incredible. They can follow Him wherever He may go, though He wanders far afield, into heathen countries, on long and aimless journeys, into desert places, where it seems there is nothing to be done. At last, in the midst of the time

when depression and anxiety are deepest; when the
enemy has grown in strength and the homage of the
people has visibly cooled; when He Himself is hiding in
voluntary exile; when He has resumed His old affection
for hiddenness and prayer; when miracles have almost
ceased, nay when, as at Bethsaida, the very power of
working miracles seems to be deserting Him; at that
moment, with all else taken from Him, and His pure self
standing stark before them, He puts them to the test. At
such a moment He asks them, as it were, to bring to a
focus all they have seen, and heard, and learnt about
Him, and, with the light of grace to guide them, to declare
who He is. It was in such circumstances as these, after
such training as this, that Simon Peter could say, in the
name of them all:

Thou art the Christ
The Son of the Living God.

Nevertheless all the time, at this tremendous climax
no less than at any other moment, He remains to them
the Man Jesus, the same weak being whom they had
fed over in Samaria, whom they had rescued from the
mob in Capharnaum, who had fallen asleep among them
in their little ship. Son of God though they have declared
Him, He is still in need of their help. They will protect
Him; He is theirs, and shall not be taken from them.
Though troubles threaten, though He Himself foretells
them, these gallant little Twelve will gather round Him
and shield Him from all harm. Their confession has
made them seem so strong, His familiarity has made Him
so weak, that they can almost patronise Him; these
doughty would-be heroes have yet much to learn. The
kingdom of which they shall be princes is not of the sort
they fancy in their dreams; it will not be advanced by
such methods. Rather they will be those of a child's
simplicity, even as were His own; of forgiveness and
endurance, even as He endured and forgave; of love, and
the sacrifice entailed by love, no matter what the cost.
Such begins to be their new school of training, once the
test of faith has been successfully passed. And in the
light of these lessons they follow Him, and watch Him in
His last campaign, in His last assault upon the Holy
City; fighting His way, as it were, through the armed
ranks of His enemies to His throne and His crown on

Calvary; teaching His sublimest doctrine, never more sublime than now, as He wins through, parrying every blow, defying every intrigue, denouncing and exposing His antagonists, reducing them to silence, even while He still invites them to Him, and weeps at the foresight of their doom. For in spite of the denunciation, never is He more tender than during this period of battle, never more homely, never more considerate for others, never more lavish of affection. It is as if at the end His whole human nature were striving, under the pressure of opposition, to express itself as it had never expressed itself before.

III.   THE IMPRESSION

All this would have been observed, often openly and consciously, sometimes with that subconscious influence which is a consequence of friendship, by those whom He had 'chosen Himself, that they might be with Him', the men whom in a special way He had called His friends. Day by day, as the years passed, the lines of the portrait would have been deepened; let us try to trace those lines, as they were added, one by one. They would see, first, one whom their earliest master, John the Baptist, could call 'the Lamb of God'; yet was He not so far removed from them but they could seek His company, and sit in quiet with Him through an afternoon on their first day of meeting. This Man from Nazareth, this son of Joseph, this 'Lamb of God', could join in the rejoicings at a marriage feast, yet a few days later could be filled with indignation at the desecration of the Temple, which He dared to call His 'Father's house'. He could sit through the weary night instructing a refined but timid Pharisee, through the weary afternoon with a low and somewhat brazen woman of Samaria; both were the same to Him. He would heal alike a high official's son, and a loathsome beggar at a city gate; He would choose for His companions 'whom He would Himself', with no regard to caste or convention; not even to that convention which demanded that a teacher of the law should be also one learned in the law. To stop the tears of an unknown widow He would overrule death itself; to stop the tears of a shameless woman He would risk His own good name. He would dine alike with Pharisees and with publicans, with unkempt Galilæans and the noblesse of

Bethania, equally at home with them all, making them all equally at home with Him.

Thus would the conception of the Son of Joseph broaden out, till it became that of one to whom all the world, and every type of man and woman in it, was an object of all-embracing sympathy and love. Thus would the carpenter of Nazareth become one whose workshop was creation, and whose tools were beyond the reach of human hands. Meanwhile they would see Him among themselves, shaping their lives, drawing them upward to share His life with Him. He would stimulate them to unceasing labour, yet would He set them an example of unceasing prayer. He would bid them go forth and preach the kingdom, with His authority and in His name ; yet should any preach without authority He would not prevent them. But let them preach by deed even more than by word ; let them teach not only what He taught, but in that all-embracing way in which He taught it. Hence they would watch Him, a man with men, with women an enduring and sympathetic woman, with the aged understanding and old, with children a confiding and affectionate child. They would see Him deal with one as carefully and patiently as He dealt with thousands ; He would come down to the multitudes that sought Him, let Himself be harassed by them, as they pressed upon Him in the streets, or crowded noisily about the house in which He rested, or filled to suffocation the very room in which He sat. Yet, when the choice and opportunity were given Him, always would He prefer the delights of solitude, on the hillside in the morning before men were awake, in desert places when they threatened Him, or when His own were weary: 'Come with me to a desert place, and rest awhile.' They would see Him stirred to wrath, curse and threaten malice with noble and scathing indignation, yet would He put no limits to His forgiveness and friendship for any kind of sinner.

They watch Him through it all, these Galilæan fishermen, and they wonder. The miracles make them question among themselves: 'Who is this ? For the wind and the sea obey him', but the personality of the Man in their midst strikes deeper down than the miracles. So preoccupied is He with the work He has to do, with the will of the Father and the spreading of the Gospel of the kingdom, with the teaching of the fact of the Son of Man and an appeal that embraced all the world ; yet is He no visionary, lost in dreams, but is patient to attend to the needs of every day, and of every single soul that comes to Him. They see Him eager that His own, His Nazarenes, His Galilæans, His Judæans, His lost sheep of the house of Israel, should receive Him first of all, yet, a strange thing to them however natural to Him, when He is rejected He passes on elsewhere, finding consolation in any ' little ones ' whatever that will receive Him. None is more observant of the law than He, yet with the authority of a lawmaker He pours scorn on those who worshipped only the letter. Instead, absolutely, irresistibly, He teaches His own law, with His commanding: ' I say to you.' Yet He knew well, and deferred to, those who de-murred, and resented, and questioned. He stood among them uniquely strong, relying on none but Himself, whether before friend or foe ; yet none more tender when occasion called for it, with a weeping widow, with a help-less outcast, with one crushed down by shame, with a maid that was dead raised to life, with old age bent double, with children standing at His knee. They heard Him, as they had not heard even their leader John the Baptist, demanding faith in Himself, smiling encourage-ment whenever a sign of it appeared, rewarding it when it was entire with reward pressed down and flowing over, stirring it when it hesitated, driving, rebuking, appealing, promising, threatening, never so disappointed, never so seemingly impatient as when the faith of man faltered.

They witnessed Him, standing alone in the Temple court, defiant of His enemies, unflinching in spite of them, firm, fearless, and no man dared to lay hands on Him. They followed Him among the crowds, and beheld His universal manner ; frank and equal with the great and mighty, homely and simple with those of low degree ; beloved and admired by saints ; sought for and trusted by sinners ; to the simple easily transparent, yet remain-ing an enigma to the learned, still more to men of guile ; winning men of good will by a mere look, a word, a single act, while evil-minded men saw nothing ; calm and self-possessed in His friendships, at times even to stern-ness in spite of His manifest love, yet He could weep for one who was dead, and when His own hour came could break down in fear and appeal for support ; from the beginning knowing what would be, neglect, contempt, mistrust, misunderstanding, hatred, failure, persecution, rejection, treachery, insult, mockery, tortures, death, yet to the end never wavering, finding excuse for those who did Him wrong, trusting on, loving to the end, forgiving and again forgiving.

They watched this Man and lived with Him, and the solemn truth grew upon them that He was more than man. This Man was true, in Himself and in His every word; He could not deceive, nor could He be deceived, above all when He spoke of Himself. He was indeed what the Baptist had said of Him, the 'Lamb of God', the King that was to come, who would baptise with fire and the Holy Ghost. He was what He declared Himself to be, the very Son of the Father, the Son of God before Abraham, one with the Father, God. This Man was indeed 'Christ the Son of the Living God'. So as the months passed by these Twelve were trained to see. And they gave witness of what they saw, and in the light of that witness we live.

> That which was from the beginning
> Which we have heard
> Which we have seen with our eyes
> Which we have looked upon
> And our hands have handled
> Of the word of life.

> That which we have seen and heard
> We declare unto you
> That you also may have fellowship with us
> And our fellowship may be with the Father
> And with His Son Jesus Christ.

VII

JESUS, MASTER OF LANGUAGE

IT has often been remarked how perfectly the four
Gospels combine simplicity of diction with absolute
fidelity; even those who will not accept them as
historical documents will concede their *naïveté*, their
absence of all attempt either to disguise or ornate their
tale. St. Luke speaks for them all when he writes: ' It
seemed good to me, having diligently attained to all
things from the beginning, to write to thee in order, most
excellent Theophilus, that thou mayest know the verity of
those words in which thou hast been instructed ' ; and
posterity has accepted his declaration as utterly sincere,
confirmed by the internal evidence of all he has written.
One has heard the story of the Annunciation, as St. Luke
has told it, declared by a master of criticism to be the
most perfect historical narrative that has ever been told ;
with not a word too much, not a word too little, add to
it or subtract from it and it is at once spoilt. But it is
the same with the rest of the early pictures of St. Luke.
It is not belief in Christianity alone that makes his account
of the Nativity always new and alive ; it is just the
narrative itself, the simple coming in and going out of
the characters concerned, of Mary and Joseph, of the
angels and the shepherds, that secures its immortality as
long as literature shall have any meaning. It is the same
with St. Matthew's story of the Magi, the same again with
St. Luke's picture of the Finding in the Temple ; man
may believe them as true narratives or not, they cannot
deny the perfection with which they are told. And yet
behind this fidelity to truth, characteristic of the evangelists, which has put their four Gospels among the greatest
books that men have ever written, there is a still more
impressive picture of Him whom they set out to describe,
and from whom they learnt their handling of words. As
with a palimpsest, rub out Matthew, and Mark, and Luke.

and John, precious as they are, and there remains Jesus Christ, master of and more perfect than them all, whose use of language, apart from what He taught, we would maintain to be without parallel in the history of the whole world's literature. It is not that Jesus was an orator in the accepted sense of the schools ; we have no evidence that He ever wrote anything, except once with His finger on the ground ; what He said, and the way He said it, did not come from any human training, for His enemies could ask with perfect truth: ' How doth this man know letters, having never learnt ? ' It was just that perfection of diction, that perfect use of words, adapted to that which He had to say, and to those to whom He said it, and to the circumstances in which it was said, which puts Him in the first place among men of letters, even if we consider Him as Man and no more. ' Never did man speak as this man spoke ', was said of Him in that centre of learning, Jerusalem ; and we may add, without fear of serious contradiction, never has any man spoken since as He has spoken. Nay, more ; even with the example which He has set, never has any man succeeded in perfectly imitating Him. We can imitate Demosthenes, a student is taught to reproduce the language of Cicero and Virgil ; Jesus Christ is inimitable, we are content to quote His words, knowing well that they stand alone.

First there is the directness even of His ordinary speech. There is never a word too much or too little ; never any needless explanation ; if explanation is needed He will usually suggest it by a question, leaving His hearer to supply the answer for himself. Thus to His mother: ' How is it that you sought me ? Did you not know that I must be about my Father's business ? ' To the Pharisee Nicodemus: ' Art thou a master in Israel, and knowest not these things ? ' To His first disciples who are waiting that they may learn: ' Do not you say: There are yet four months, and then the harvest cometh ? Behold I say to you, lift up your eyes and see the countries, for they are white for the harvest.' To His critics on the first great occasion that He faces them, and indeed regularly after: ' How can you believe, who receive glory from one another: and the glory which is from God alone you do not seek ? ' These are enough for explanations. There is no argument, no waste in discussion ; He is so sure, that He can leave both His friends and His enemies to answer

the questions for themselves. Instead, when He has anything definite to say, His sentences are uttered short and
sharp, like the crack of a whip or the hit of a hammer.
' I will, be thou made clean.'   ' Be of good heart, Son,
thy sins are forgiven thee.'   ' I say to thee, Arise, take up
thy bed, and go into thy house.'   ' Come, follow me.'   They
ring out clearly from the beginning to the end of His
life ; even when He is questioned there is no hesitation,
the answer is always prompt and definite.   But most
definite of all are His illustrations.   He seizes on whatever is before His eyes, and at once turns it to account.
He sees a tattered garment :   ' No man putteth a piece
from a new garment upon an old garment: otherwise he
both rendeth the new, and the piece taken from the new
agreeth not with the old '.   He sees men drinking outside
a tavern: ' No man drinking old wine hath presently a
mind to new: for he saith: The old is better.'   He hears
the Pharisees complaining of this thing or that ;   to
Pharisees, who thought in terms of the Old Testament,
He answers almost invariably in the same: ' Have you
not read what David did when he was hungry and they
that were with him ?   How he entered into the house of
God, and did eat the loaves of proposition, which it was
not lawful for him to eat, nor those that were with him,
but for the priests only ? '   He speaks to the country
people on their own hillside, and at once His language is
attuned to them ; to the sufferings and trials of their own
humble lives, to the high reward that awaits them beyond
that of the scribes and Pharisees, if only they will avoid
the evils that are common among them, their quarrelling
with one another, their calling each other names, their un-
forgivingness, their tendency to coarse vices, their in-
clination to take scandal from each other, their looseness
in cursing and swearing, their exacting of the last farthing
from one who has done them wrong.   So true is He to the
life before Him that it would not be difficult, from His
words alone, to paint a true picture of the lives and characters of the poor country folk of Galilee.   When in the
Sermon on the Mount He has told them plainly of their
faults, and has lifted them up to higher ideals by means
of the things they have about them, making use even of
the very grass beneath their feet, ' which is to-day, and
to-morrow is cast into the oven ', or to the crows above
their heads ' which sow not, neither do they reap, neither

have they storehouse nor barn, and God feedeth them ',
we do not wonder that His hearers, dull and untutored as
they were, followed every word, and at the end ' were in
admiration at his doctrine ; for he was teaching them as
one having power, and not as their scribes '.

It would be an endless task, however pleasant, to follow
up this study of the way Jesus draws His illustrations
immediately from those to whom He speaks, and from the
conditions of the place around Him ; to country people
from country experience, to dwellers in cities from the
things they have most at heart, to the rich by means of
money and merchandise, to the learned in the law by
the Scriptures. But we must pass this by for the
still more wonderful way He invents and makes use
of stories. They are always at hand, always suited
to His audience, always complete, with not a word too
much or too little. He speaks at the table of a wealthy
Pharisee, with other wealthy Pharisees present ; and His
story is of one who lent money, complete in two short
sentences, yet with the moral so clear that no one can
fail to answer the question He puts to them in conclusion.
He meets them again when they suggest that He casts
out devils by Beelzebub, and in a single sentence He
reminds them of the fate of a city divided against itself ;
fit illustration for these arch-plotters, who at that very
moment were combining with their rivals the Sadducees,
with their political opponents the Herodians, to destroy
Him. The story of the sower who went forth to sow his
seed, and the fate that seed met, is the story of almost
every man that was listening to Him that evening on the
lake-side ; the series that followed, of wheat sown and
the cockle amongst it, of the grain of mustard-seed growing to a tree by the side of the cottage, of the leaven
thrown into the meal by the housewife who baked her
bread, of the treasure-trove, of the precious stone, all
these were interests of every-day life to the people of
that time and place. At the end of them all, when He
has given to His disciples their explanation, He describes
Himself and His manner when He says: ' Have ye understood all these things ? They say to him: Yes. He said
unto them: Therefore every scribe instructed in the
kingdom of heaven is like to a man that is a householder,
that bringeth out of his treasure new things and old.'

Or, again, to show the ease with which He enters into

the very souls of those to whom He speaks, watch the
lightning flashes of His sympathy. When He compas-
sionates His words are very few, but they are always to
the point and perfect. 'Be of good heart, Son, thy sins
are forgiven thee.' 'And seeing her, he had compassion
on her, and he said to her: Weep not.' 'And he said to
the woman: Thy faith hath made thee safe, go in peace.'
'He that doth the will of my Father who is in heaven,
he is my brother, and my sister, and my mother.'
'Daughter, thy faith hath made thee safe ; go in peace,
and be thou whole of thy disease.' 'And seeing the multitudes, he had compassion on them: because they were
distressed, and lying like sheep that have no shepherd.
Then he saith to his disciples: The harvest indeed is
great but the labourers are few. Pray ye therefore the
Lord of the harvest, that he send forth labourers into his
harvest.'

With such delicate tenderness, with no waste of words,
with not a shadow of sentiment, is His sympathy proved.
And it is never weakness. On the contrary, even in
His most sympathetic moments, there is command and
authority in every word He says. We have seen it in His
words to His mother, to the widow of Naim, to the
woman with the issue of blood ; when later He is taking
His rest in the house of Martha and Mary, it is the same:
'Martha, Martha, thou art troubled about many things.
But one thing is necessary' ; and there the story ends, as
if there were no more to be said. He has compassion on
the multitude, but He never yields to it. In the desert,
out of pity, after He has been with them all the day, He
feeds 5,000 men, with their women and children. He is
hailed as 'the Prophet' ; they wish there and then to
make him King ; at once the sympathy of Jesus, though
it does not abate, rises above it all, and with a word of
command He dismisses, first the disciples to their boat,
and then the multitude to their rest. Next day it is the
same. He comes amongst them again in the synagogue at
Capharnaum. At first they are enthusiastic ; they wish
to hear Him, to receive from Him the bread which He
promises. He does not hesitate ; He offers them more
and more, gently, suited to their understanding if they
choose to take what He says, but none the less firmly and
without compromise. They fail Him, but He does not
retract ; they leave Him, and 'walk with Him no more',

but He shows no anger; He is content to turn to those who still stand by Him and ask them: 'Will you also go away?'

This same sympathy, combined with authority, He shows especially in His dealings with His enemies; indeed, in general it is in His attitude to them that His power of language appears most manifest. We have seen the firm, emphatic stand He took on His first encounter with them, answering them with the challenge, fired like a shot of a pistol: 'Destroy this temple, and in three days I will raise it up again'. Nevertheless, almost immediately after, He is all patient; but patient again with authority in every word He speaks, when He receives a Pharisee by night: 'Art thou a teacher in Israel, and knowest not these things?' We have seen Him again in the Temple court, harried because He had healed an aged beggar on the sabbath. His defence is a long one, but every sentence rings out distinct in itself, like the shots of a machine-gun, full of feeling, full no less of command: 'My Father worketh until now, and I also work.—Search the scriptures, since you think that in them you have eternal life; these are they that give witness of me.—If you believed in Moses, you would believe in me; for he wrote concerning me.' As with the Galilæans, so with these men of the Temple; they lived upon the Scriptures, Jesus appeals to them in their own language.

So it had been always; when, then, He inveighed against them, because they complained of His eating with publicans and sinners, that He presumed to forgive sin, that His disciples plucked ears of corn on the sabbath, that He worked miracles on the sabbath day, that He permitted a sinful woman to touch Him; when He showed anger because they said that He cast out devils by Beelzebub, the prince of devils, or because they took scandal at His disciples eating with unwashed hands; when they pestered Him for a sign, and yet a further sign, and yet another, and He would give them no more, calling them to their faces, 'a wicked and adulterous generation'; when He warned His disciples to beware of their leaven, for that it was nothing more than hypocrisy; on all these occasions it is manifest that the Pharisees themselves knew very well the exact balance of the language He used. His angry words are not from ill-temper, no one ever accused Him of that. His charges against them are never denied, they may hate Him for what He said, but they do not refute Him. His vehemence against them is never misconstrued into impatience ; always, when they can be, they are in His company, 'watching Him ', questioning, examining, presuming on that very compassion which is manifest in Him all the time.

Hence, as the end draws nearer, it is in the presence of the enemy, the scribes and Pharisees, the priests and lawyers, that His human eloquence seems to flash out in all its brilliance. They may ask, in order to depreciate Him : ' How doth this man know letters, having never learnt ? ' The very question confesses that they were listening to one who was their master. They might send their police to silence Him, and to take Him prisoner ; the police could only return saying : ' Never did man speak as this man speaketh.' They might hope to test Him by bringing before Him a woman taken in sin ; a single word from Him, and they slink away. On the other hand, with a vividness of diction that stirred the people to their very depths, Jesus describes Himself before them all : ' I am the light of the world. He that followeth me walketh not in darkness, but shall have the light of life —When you shall have lifted up the Son of Man, then shall you know that I am—Amen, amen I say to you, before Abraham was born I am—Amen, amen I say to you, I am the door of the sheep—I am the good shepherd, and I know mine and mine know me.' ' He hath a devil and is mad ; why listen to him ? ' was all His enemies could say ; and they received in answer, from the common crowd : ' These are not the words of a madman '. They were not, indeed ; sublime as they were, they rang true. And as if to show how perfectly Jesus had control, both of Himself and of those who accused Him, listen to Him immediately after, pouring out His soul in language worthy of the finest poet : ' Come to me all you that labour and are heavily burthened, and I will refresh you. Take my yoke upon you, and learn of me, because I am meek and humble of heart, and you shall find rest for your souls. For my yoke is sweet and my burden light.' It is in answer to a master in the law, who put a question to tempt Him, that He told the story of the Good Samaritan, that masterpiece of dramatic narrative, each of its four characters crossing the stage with the perfect rhythm of a perfect play. It is in reply to some who again

brought up against Him the charge of Beelzebub, that
He retorts with the weird picture of the demons cast out,
and returning at last to the soul from which they had
come. It is apparently to testing critics that He gives the
beautiful comparison: 'The light of thy body is thy eye.
If thy eye be single, thy whole body will be lightsome;
but if it be evil thy body also will be darksome. Take
heed therefore that the light which is in thee be not
darkness.' Mark the conclusion of this discourse; it
proves the sweetness of the Master's words, even while
they spare no evil: 'And as he was speaking, a certain
Pharisee prayed him that he would dine with him. And
he going in, sat down to eat.' Or if He finds others, scribes
or Pharisees though they be, more willing to listen to
Him, He will describe them to themselves in language
that cannot be mistaken. Seated at table with them, He
will warn them against seeking the first places, lest they
be decried and made to sit lower. With the rich and
prosperous He will tell of one whose granaries were full,
and who thought of building more, but God that night
required his soul of him. He will ask them why, if they
could read the skies and the clouds, and could foretell
the weather that would come, they failed to read the signs
of the times in which they were living; why if He did
the works of His Father, they refused to believe, not
Himself, but the works that He did. He will bid them,
when they give a banquet, not to forget 'the poor, the
maimed, the lame, and the blind; and thou shalt be
blessed, because they have not wherewith to make thee
recompense: for recompense shall be made thee at the
resurrection of the just'. He will warn them against
making excuses when the Father calls them, just those
excuses which these men of the world had at the moment
uppermost in their minds. If they hesitate, if they hang
back in fear or in despair, He will remind them of their
own efforts to save a single lost sheep out of a hundred, of
the joy of the woman who has lost and found her penny,
of the Father's welcome given to his son who had wandered far away. And if even this will not move them, if
there is need, after all this proof of sympathy and love,
still to stir them by fear, He will tell them of the rich
man who here on earth was clothed in purple and fine
linen, yet afterwards was buried in hell; and of the poor
man in rags, whose sores the dogs licked, yet was found

in the end in the bosom of Abraham. Thus in the closing
months it is very noticeable how eloquent is His appeal,
no longer in the simple language and imagery of the
Galilæan countryfolk, but in that of the Judæan
Pharisees. They ask Him when the kingdom of God
shall come ; He replies that it will come like lightning,
and recalls to their minds the flood that overwhelmed men
in the days of Noe, and the fire that burnt up Sodom in
the days of Lot. They pride themselves on their prayer ;
He shows them the Pharisee praying whose prayer is not
heard, the sinful publican who prays and is justified.
They seek to catch Him with a question about divorce ;
He refers them to their own law, and then adds His own.
Then once more, as if He would make a final appeal to
win them, He tells them the story of the Master who
hired workers for his vineyard at all hours of the day,
yet at the end would reward the last even as he gave to
the first. In Jericho, the rich man's city, the city of the
merchants, and bankers, and money-lenders, where the
trade of the East converged before it went to or from
Jerusalem, after He had shown His affection for a chief
publican, He pronounced that parable of the Talents,
which has given the very word a new meaning for the
rest of time. In the influence of that word alone one may
judge of the influence of Jesus Christ as a Master of
words ; has it any precise parallel in the whole history of
literature ?

We come now to the last phase, in which the whole
character, and especially the power, of Christ is portrayed
in all its glory, as it is nowhere else in the Gospels. It
opens with a word of command, that the Master had need
of the ass tethered at the roadside. There is no remonstrance ; the word has come from one whom, by this time,
it has grown to be natural for all to obey. There follows
the Procession of Palms ; during that Procession He
speaks twice, once with that authority which again rings
out like the shot of a rifle, once with that pathos, combined with authority, which rolls like a distant clap of
thunder, echoing across the skies. To the Pharisees who
complain He replies : ' I say to you, that if these shall
hold their peace, the stones will cry out ' ; but at the
sight of the doomed city, ' He wept over it, saying: If
thou also hadst known, and that in this thy day, the things
that are to thy peace ! But now they are hidden from thy

eyes. For the days shall come upon thee: and thy enemies shall cast a trench about thee, and compass thee round, and straighten thee on every side, and beat thee flat to the ground, and thy children who are in thee. And they shall not leave in thee a stone upon a stone: because thou hast not known the time of thy visitation.' One may search in vain through the sublimest of the prophet-poets for poetry so perfect as this, so poignant, so real in its matter, its circumstances, and its rendering. It is akin to *King Lear;* it surpasses *King Lear* in the vividness and terror of the tragedy.

With authority and tenderness thus emphasised at the outset, Jesus passes through the week displaying at every turn His mastery of dialectic. He has before Him the subtlest questioners in the world ; at every turn He beats them with their own weapons. They question Him ; He asks a counter-question and they are silenced. He draws a picture of cruelty and injustice which compels them to pass sentence and condemn ; almost before the words have passed their lips they realise that they have condemned themselves. Pharisees set before Him a case of conscience, and Sadducees rejoice at their discomfiture ; Sadducees, and the Pharisees are satisfied no less ; scribes, and they, too, are silenced, so that ' no one any longer dared to ask him further questions '. Then, when He has humbled them, He turns to the attack ; and by a single question, drawn from the Scriptures whose interpretation they alone were considered able to give, He so confounded them that ' no one was able to answer Him a word '. We are reminded of that first scene, twenty years before, when a boy of twelve sat ' in the midst of the doctors, hearing them and asking them questions, and all that heard him were astonished at his wisdom and his answers '. When He has done all this, when with patience unbroken He has appealed to them through the years, when He has received and rewarded every sign of recognition from any individual among them, when He has presented His credentials to them in word and in deed, when He has shown them their error in ways that they could not deny, when He has refuted their charges every one, when He has offered them all that a God-man could offer if they would but accept Him, when He has made them condemn themselves, and they have been put to shame in their own eyes by their manifest extravagances, when He has made them see for themselves the wickedness and adultery of their generation, when in spite of all this they have refused to receive Him, only then, in an unsurpassed peroration which Demosthenes or Cicero would have rejoiced to call his own, does He pronounce their doom: ' Woe to you, scribes and Pharisees, hypocrites ! '

It is worth while looking at that peroration ; in construction as well as in subject-matter it is a masterpiece of oratory. First He gives the scribes and Pharisees their due, addressing not them but the people about Him ; no one shall say that He is disloyal or teaches disloyalty. The scribes and Pharisees represent the law ; therefore in their teaching of the law let them be obeyed. Next, still addressing the people, He sums up in a short introduction what He is about to elaborate. It is not their words, but their works which He condemns. They impose insupportable burthens ; they make show of their sanctity that they may be seen by men ; they seek the first places and the highest honours ; let their disciples know that in all this they are not to be followed. Then He turns to the scribes and Pharisees themselves, and in concrete examples brings home to them the evil of their ways.

' Woe to you scribes and Pharisees, hypocrites, because you shut the kingdom of heaven against men.

' Woe to you scribes and Pharisees, hypocrites, because you devour the houses of widows, while you pray long prayers.

' Woe to you scribes and Pharisees, hypocrites, because you move heaven and earth to convert one proselyte, only to make him a worse child of hell than yourselves.

' Woe to you scribes and Pharisees, hypocrites, because you tax mint and cummin, yet have neglected judgement and mercy and faith.

' Woe to you scribes and Pharisees, hypocrites, because you make clean the outside of the cup, but within you are full of rapine and uncleanness.

' Woe to you scribes and Pharisees, hypocrites, because you are like to whited sepulchres, which outwardly appear to men beautiful, but within are full of dead men's bones and all filthiness.

' Woe to you scribes and Pharisees, hypocrites, because you build the sepulchres of the prophets and honour them, yet are you the sons of them that killed them.

'You serpents, generation of vipers, how will you flee from the judgement of hell ? '

So the accusations succeed one another, the imagery growing in vividness as the charge progresses. There are pauses here and there, parenthesis to mark the contrast between what is and what should be ; but always the oratory returns to its point, and strikes with a force that nothing can resist. Then there is a pause ; the orator Himself is, as it were, overcome by the picture He has been compelled to paint. He sees what must happen in the future from all this ; suffering and death to His own, death and destruction to the city that has been the home of such men. ' Behold I send to you prophets and wise men and scribes: and some of them you will put to death and crucify ; and some you will scourge in your syna-gogues and persecute from city to city.' ' Jerusalem, Jerusalem, thou that killest the prophets, and stonest them that are sent to thee, how often would I have gathered together thy children, as the hen doth gather her chickens under her wings, and thou wouldest not ! Behold your home shall be left to you desolate.'

It is a perfect rhetorical conclusion. Jesus has risen to the full height of His indignation. He has spared His enemies in nothing, though He knows full well what the consequences must be for Himself. Yet of Himself, from beginning to end, there has not been a word ; He sees only the suffering that must come to those He loves, the doom that must come to His enemies, and His great heart breaks in grief, expressing itself once more in the language of perfect poetry, which a Shakespeare cannot surpass. In the Sermon on the Mount He has shown Himself the perfect Teacher ; in the Parables He has proved His supreme power of dramatic narrative ; in the Sermon on the Blessed Sacrament He has given a perfect lesson in the art of drawing an audience to the highest contemplation ; in the swift way He has employed the things about Him, a child, a man at work, a woman in her cottage, an ox and a mule, a sheep and a goat, the birds of the air and flower on the road-side, men drinking at the wineshop and others clinking money in the market-place, texts and scenes of scripture and lessons of the law, He has shown His supreme readiness of illustration. In this address to the scribes and Pharisees He proves His unsurpassed skill in invective, made the more perfect because it ends, not on a note of anger, but on one of deepest sympathy and pity. Never, we would claim, has so much variety in the use of language, and that in its perfection, been found before or since in a single man.

There is no need to pursue this study further, though in the closing scenes there is much to learn. To the Jews of that time apocalyptic literature had a peculiar fascination; on the hill of Olivet Jesus used the apocalyptic manner in a way that makes the style of an Ezechiel or a Daniel grow pale. It was all mystery, it is all mystery still; yet does it ring true in every detail, and the coming of the Son of Man, with His cry: 'Come ye blessed of my Father, possess the kingdom prepared for you from the beginning of the world', is a picture which has in no way faded with the passing of the ages. The world will come to an end; it will end sooner than man expects; its end will be sudden; we listen to Him now as man listened to Him then, and through all the mystery and imagery we know He has given us a foreshadowing of the truth. Nor need we dwell on that wonderful eloquence of the heart displayed in the address in the Supper-room. Even there His imagery cannot leave Him; while He begins to pour out His life's blood, He is still the vine and His disciples are the branches, Simon shall be sifted as wheat, in His Father's house there are many mansions, His disciples shall suffer, but their sorrow shall be turned into joy, even as a mother's sorrow is made joy when her child is born. While He deals with life and death, His language never loses its colour, not even when in the Garden He speaks of the chalice of distress which He must drink.

The Passion shows His mastery in another way; if elsewhere He has proved His economy of words, saying never too much and never too little, here we have Him deliberately silent, conquering by His silence, using words only when duty or right demands. He welcomes the traitor by his name; He has not been deceived. He commands the crowd before He submits to it; to Annas, the unlawful judge, He replies not a word; to Caiaphas, who had the right to ask, He answers with all the dignity of a King. A soldier strikes Him, and He asks why. A disciple denies Him, and for him a look is enough. Herod tries Him and again, because he had no jurisdiction, Jesus has for him no reply; Pilate tries Him, and in every interview it is Jesus and not Pilate who is master and judge. For the rest all is silence, only when on the way to death He meets a sorrowing crowd does His beauty of language break out: 'Daughters of Jerusalem, weep not over me ; but weep for yourselves and for your children. For behold the days shall come, wherein they will say: Blessed are the barren, and the wombs that have not borne, and the breasts that have not given suck. Then shall they begin to say to the mountains: Fall upon us ; and to the hills: Cover us. For if in the green wood they do these things, what shall be done in the dry ? ' The closing lament of a tragedy of Euripides or Sophocles is not more eloquent or touching than this ; and this is made the more piercing because it is uttered in the streets of Jerusalem, not on the stage of a theatre.

Jesus is dead, and the voice is silenced. Then, like music beginning first with a murmur in the distance, it begins to be heard again: 'The voice of my beloved, Behold he cometh leaping upon the mountains, skipping over the hills.' At first it is just 'All hail ! ' ; then the use of the simple word: 'Mary ! ' Gradually it rises to a question, then an address, then an encouragement, till it reaches the old familiarity: ' Simon, Son of John, lovest thou me ? ' When that is done, then the voice ends with a thunder worthy of the Master of all men and of all language: ' All power is given to me in heaven and in earth. Going therefore, teach ye all nations: baptising them in the name of the Father and of the Son and of the Holy Ghost. Teaching them to observe all things whatsoever I have commanded you. And behold I am with you all days, even to the consummation of the world.'

This is mastery of language indeed ; a mastery which only one Man in all the history of men has dared to use. And He has been heard.

VIII

JESUS, MASTER OF MEN

THERE is one characteristic of Jesus Christ Our Lord which not only places Him above all other men in history, but establishes Him as One whose story could never have been invented; it is His unique attitude towards, and accepted mastery of, other men. He came into the world in the same manner as the rest; He had a genealogy like others, which, like that of all others, was by no means without flaw; He descended from David, it is true, but long before His time the prerogative and leadership belonging to that name had been lost in the common stream. There were still a few who remembered; there were more who looked for the day when the Messias would be born; but to them all, it would seem, the idea of the Messias was, as it were, separated from that of ordinary men. He would be great; He would be the Son of the Most High; He would sit upon the throne of David His Father, and of His Kingdom there would be no end. The Child that would be born of Mary would be of the Holy Ghost, therefore His name would be called Emmanuel, that is, God with us. In all this it was the power of the Most High that was foretold and looked for; in whatever form, from whatever place He came, He would be clothed in that majesty which had surrounded the triumphant God since the wondrous days of Sinai.

Yet when He did come it was not this majesty which was His earthly greatness; the Child of Bethlehem, the Child in the hands of Simeon, the Child hidden away in Egypt and Nazareth, had little about Him of the 'greatness' which men had hoped to see. Only those who looked from another angle, the angle of humanity itself, could have divined from the first that He was, and that from the first He assumed the rôle of, the Master of mankind. At the age of twelve we hear Him begin to speak ; they are the words of one who must command, even while He must be the model of subjection. He has been lost and found ; in the circumstances one might have expected that the father, not the mother, would have asked: ' Why hast thou done so to us ? Behold thy mother and I have sought thee sorrowing.' But no ; the father has already learnt, somehow, that he is not first ; that with this Son the mother alone must deal. And even she must learn, what she had known from the beginning, but now with final emphasis ; this Son of hers must be Master, for He had a Master's work to do: ' Did you not know that I must be about my Father's business ? '

It was an emphatic word of command, even though it is followed by the statement that He ' went down with them and came to Nazareth, and was subject to them '. And as the Hidden Life began, so did it end. It was by His order that Mary and Joseph commanded Him, for eighteen years ; when the time was over it was by His order that John baptised Him as a common sinner: ' But John stayed him, saying: I ought to be baptised by thee, and comest thou to me ? And Jesus answering, said to him: Suffer it to be so now. For so it becometh us to fulfil all justice. Then he suffered him.' And as if to make it clear that this word of command shall be heard and obeyed, not only by His mother, not only by the greatest man born of woman, but also by the very powers of darkness, it is immediately followed by another: ' Begone, Satan ! For it is written: The Lord thy God shalt thou adore, and him only shalt thou serve. Then the devil left him.'

So Jesus stepped into the life of the world about Him ; there is from the first authority to command, which never left Him. Some men follow Him down a river-bank ; He turns to them and speaks ; immediately they call Him, ' Rabbi ', to which the Evangelist significantly adds: ' And that means, Master '. He is at a marriage feast ; He gives a command that, on the fact of it, is absurd ; nevertheless He is obeyed, and obedience is rewarded. He is in the Temple court in Jerusalem ; He is indignant with the sight He sees ; with a whip-cord and no more He ' drove them all out of the temple, the sheep also and the oxen ', and there is not one that ventures to resist Him ; even a Pharisee, awed by His commanding presence, comes humbly to His feet in the night. He passes thence to

Galilee to begin His work; it is begun with the conquest of a Ruler that lived in Capharnaum; with the defiant throwing down of the gauntlet to His already declared enemies in Jerusalem; with a command to devils that they shall go out of a man, so that already 'there came fear upon all; and they talked among themselves, saying: What word is this, for with authority and power he com· mandeth the unclean spirits, and they go out? And the fame of Him was published into every place of the country.'

Thus before He has yet spoken much of the kingdom He had come to found, Jesus stands in the midst of men and, from the first, has assumed the position of Leader and Master. His enemies know it and hate Him for it, before yet He has stated what He has against them; His friends know it and go after Him, believing they scarcely know what or why; the indifferent may try to ignore, nevertheless He is the talk of the whole country-side, His name is in every mouth. Now He confirms the impression; He shows that His authority is not only the greatest among men, it reaches far beyond that of all men. He meets a leper by the road: 'I will, be thou made clean; and immediately the leprosy left him'. He is shown a poor man sick of the palsy; on His own authority once more, without any appeal to heaven: 'Be of good heart, Son, thy sins are forgiven thee'; and to prove that this power is not a vain boast: 'I say to thee, arise, take up thy bed, and go into thy house. . . And all were astonished: and they glorified God. And they were filled with fear, saying: We have seen wonderful things to-day. And they glorified God that gave such power to men.' He commands a publican, seated at his counter, and turns him into a disciple; He commands the critics who complain of the doings of His followers on the sabbath day, and declares Himself 'Lord even of the sabbath'; when again they would test Him 'that they might find an accusation against him', He 'looked round about on them all', He restored to a man his withered hand, so that 'they were filled with madness: and they talked one with another, what they might do to Jesus'.

It is with such majesty as this that all the early months of the public career are marked. He has begun from Nazareth, whence nothing good could come; at once the name of Jesus of Nazareth is the centre of discussion, from Tyre and Sidon to Jerusalem. It is true that at this point, as if to preserve the balance, Matthew reminds us of the prophecy that was being fulfilled in Him: 'Behold my servant whom I have chosen, my beloved in whom my soul hath been well pleased. . . . He shall not contend nor cry out: neither shall any man hear his voice in the streets. The bruised reed he shall not break: and smoking flax he shall not extinguish'; nevertheless in that same prophecy we are told that 'the spirit of the Lord' would be upon Him, that He would 'show judgement to the Gentiles', that He would 'send forth judgement unto victory', that 'in his name the Gentiles would hope'. Already the multitude had learnt whom they could trust and obey, already the disciples knew whom they could believe and follow, already the enemy were well aware whom they must thwart even, if it must be, by compassing His death. The first part of the career of Jesus had been spent in establishing this mastery among men.

And now, with this majesty established, we see Him acting indeed 'as one having authority, and not as the scribes'. He goes up into a mountain and calls His followers about Him; out of these He chooses twelve, 'whom he would himself', 'that they might be with him, and that he might send them to preach, and might have power to cast out devils'. That work done, He comes down to the people, 'and opening his mouth he spoke to them'. He gave them new standards of blessedness, such as had never been heard of before. He gave them new standards of morals: 'I say to you', was His authority, superseding Moses and the Law. He spoke to them of prayer, and of the manner of prayer: 'Thus shall you pray', as one who was Master even of the realm of prayer. Nay, more, He was indeed its Master; for 'Not every one that saith to me, Lord, Lord, shall enter into the kingdom of heaven: but he that doth the will of my Father who is in heaven, he shall enter into the kingdom of heaven'. It was the climax of His day: 'And it came to pass, when Jesus had fully ended these words, the people were in admiration at his doctrine. For he was teaching them as one having power, and not as the scribes and Pharisees'. 'Not as the scribes and Pharisees'; once He had shown how He excelled them in word, He must show how He excelled them in deed. They chafed under the yoke of Rome, and had no love for its officials ; He must choose a Roman soldier and must say of him that He had not found such faith in all Israel as He had found in him. They devour the substance of widows and orphans ; He must pass a mourning widow, and must raise her son to life for her comfort. They make it a law to have no dealings with a sinful woman, her shadow must not be allowed to cross them in the street ; He must be Master even of such, and when such a woman touches Him, kisses His feet in the sight of all and washes them with her tears, He must then manifest His dignity, Master of friend and critic alike in that room. The critics may pursue Him ; since He is their proved Master they may now say that His mastery came, not from God, not from men, but from Beelzebub ; He would read their thoughts, He would denounce them before all the people: ' O generation of vipers, how can you speak good things whereas you are evil ? For out of the abundance of the heart the mouth speaketh '.

When, then, at this point of His life His whole method began to change, none could say that He had been beaten, or that He had ceased to speak with authority, or that He was no longer Master of men. Henceforth, we are told, He began to speak to the people in parables ; but it was because they were failing Him, not because He had failed them. The very language in which He spoke proved that His authority was the same, all the more when He re-served to the Twelve alone the key to the mystery. The Pharisees might ask for a sign, not that they might believe but that they might further criticise ; with the dignity of the Master He refused to grant it to them. The people might follow Him with enthusiasm, because He did wonders, because He was to their profit and renown, with the dignity of true discernment He would not cast His pearls before swine. He would still have pity on them, ' because they were distressed and lying like sheep that had no shepherd ' ; therefore He would not desert them, He would still go after even one. But it was all very different now ; and when some went so far as to ' laugh him to scorn ', though He raised a dead child to life to silence them, still for a time He would leave them to themselves, for they were no longer worthy of Him. It is true He would not desert them ; He would send His twelve chosen ones to teach them in His name, with His authority, with His own power of miracles ; if they would not hear Him, let them hear them, later perhaps they would return.

Once only before the separation He would have them declare Him. He went apart to a desert place, on the north of the lake ; there followed Him great crowds, to the number of five thousand men, not counting women and children. As the day drew to evening they were hungry, and had not food to eat. With the authority of a king He bade them sit down, carefully marshalled in groups of hundreds and fifties. With a few loaves and fishes He fed them all, with His company of twelve He kept them together ; they saw what He had done, they were captivated once again. ' This is indeed the prophet that is to come into the world ', they cried, and they rose up to make Him their King. But that was enough ; at this crucial moment of His life He had compelled them to confess Him ; now with the same authority He quelled their ardour, and bade them lie down to sleep. The next day, a momentous day, on the strength of their confession, He offered them yet more, and they failed Him. ' After this many of his disciples went back, and walked no more with him ' ; not because they would not own Him for their King, but because He would not be the king that they desired ; not because He was no prophet, but because His saying was hard, and they would not hear it. In defeat as in success He was still the Master: ' Lord, to whom shall we go ? Thou hast the words of eternal life '.

We watch Him now for a time yielding to the pressure of His enemies. But it was a strong man's yielding ; even in the land of the infidel He ' went about doing good ', to the Syro-Phœnician woman, to the deaf and dumb, to the Four Thousand whom He fed in Decapolis, to the Blind Man at Bethsaida. Now more than ever He is firm against His enemies ; they ask for a sign, and a wicked and adulterous generation shall not be given it, their leaven must be avoided for it is the leaven of hypocrisy. Now more than ever He tests His own ; even in this time of seeming defeat and retirement the mastery must have appeared in magnificence to make Simon Peter declare: ' Thou art the Christ, the Son of the living God '. It met with its reward ; on Thabor a week later He was shown to them: ' The Beloved Son, in whom the Father was well pleased ', Master not only of the men among whom

He lived, but Master of the past, of Moses and Elias, and of the future, even of the Passion He was about to accomplish in Jerusalem.

But now that the great confession has been made, now that the last phase has definitely begun, the majesty of Jesus Christ shines out in greater splendour. He looks steadily to the Passion before Him; He warns His followers that soon He will permit it to be. He speaks now as though He commanded all men and everything. Do men ask for the tax? Let them have it. Do His own pride themselves beneath His shadow? Let them be as little children. Do strangers work miracles in His name? Let them do so. Would His followers know how often they must forgive? Why seventy-times seven times, and more again if it were needed. Do the Samaritans receive them badly as they pass through their country? Let them have their way; He will go elsewhere. Do some wish to follow Him, but on conditions of their own? The Son of Man hath not where to lay His head, let the dead bury their dead; no man who puts his hand to the plough and looks back is worthy of Him. The answers ring out firm and independent; they are the answers of the 'strong man armed', who is going forward to His last campaign, and must needs strengthen those whom He calls to fight with Him.

At last that campaign begins, and never more than now does His mastery of scribes and Pharisees appear. He challenges them on their own ground: 'How doth this man know letters, having never learned?' is all they can reply. 'Is not this he whom they seek to kill? And behold he speaketh openly; and they say nothing to him. Have the rulers known for a truth that this is the Christ?' So the talk begins to spread; and what could the enemy do? 'They sought therefore to apprehend him: and no man laid hands on him, because his hour was not yet come'. 'And the rulers and Pharisees sent ministers to apprehend him'; but those ministers returned empty-handed: 'Never did man speak like this man'. They are feeble cries indeed that we hear: 'We know this man whence he cometh: but when the Christ cometh, no man knoweth whence he is'. 'Are you also deceived? Hath any one of the rulers believed in him, or of the Pharisees?' 'Search the scriptures and see that out of Galilee a prophet riseth not.' 'Thou givest testimony of thyself; thy testimony is not true.' 'Do not we say well that thou art a Samaritan and hast a devil?' 'Give glory to God. We know that this man is a sinner.' 'We know that God spoke to Moses. But as to this man, we know not whence he is.' Contrast all this with that other challenge, and say which is the Master:

'I am the good shepherd: and I know mine and mine know me . and I lay down my life for my sheep. Therefore doth the Father love me: because I lay down my life that I may take it up again. No man taketh it away from me: but I lay it down of myself. And I have power to lay it down: and I have power to take it up again. This commandment have I received from my Father.'

Such is the mastery of Jesus in battle, as He stands alone on the field of the enemy's own choosing; in repose He is no less masterful. 'Come to me, all you that labour and are burdened, and I will refresh you. Take my yoke upon you, and learn of me, because I am meek and humble of heart, and you shall find rest for your souls.' Such is His word of command; when one asks for an example He tells the story of the Good Samaritan, and concludes with the sharp order: 'Go thou and do in like manner'. He is Master in the house of Martha, Master when His Twelve ask Him how to pray, Master in the streets when one praises His mother, Master at the table of the Pharisees, where at last, before their faces, the great 'Woe' begins to be heard. He is Master with those who would catch Him in His speech, who would set Him subtle questions of the law, who sought to stone Him, to kill Him, to seize Him, and He passed out of their hands He is Master of Herod and defies him: 'Go and tell that fox: Behold I cast out devils and do cures, to-day and to-morrow, and the third day I am consummated. Nevertheless I must walk to-day and to-morrow, because it cannot be that a prophet perish out of Jerusalem.' So the story goes on through these latter days; the story of one who commands His enemies, who meets their murmurs with rebuke, yet who will appeal to Jerusalem even at this last moment, will go after a single sheep that is lost, will bid His own conquer all opposition by peace, and faith, and lowliness.

Now the end comes definitely in sight; and now more than ever Jesus shows Himself the Master of men, the

Master of life and death. The enemy have made it dangerous for Him to be seen in Judæa; He crosses the Jordan in defiance of them all, that He may come to Bethania and comfort two friends, by raising their brother from the tomb. Prudence bids Him again retire for a time that He may not be seen; when that time is ended all Palestine shall see Him as He makes His last tour of farewell. It shall be marked as other tours have been marked, with acts of mercy on the one hand, with stern warnings on the other. He will heal ten lepers on the road-side, and lament that but one returns to thank Him; almost on the same spot He will warn His enquirers of the coming of the kingdom. He will still tell them parables of mercy, yet He will speak strong words against those who would tamper with the sacred bond of marriage. He will have children brought to Him and He will bless them, 'for of such is the kingdom of heaven'. Yet a rich young man will come to Him, asking for the true way to perfection; Jesus will not mince matters, He is strong to all alike: 'And Jesus, looking on him, loved him and said to him: One thing is wanting to thee. If thou wouldst be perfect go, sell whatsoever thou hast and give it to the poor, and thou shalt have treasure in heaven. And come, follow me.'

In this way, to the very end, the Master has been manifest. In the earliest days He was subject to Mary and Joseph; yet even then there was something about Him which made them pause when they did not understand. The Baptist had understood better, and had been prepared to pay Him all reverence; yet even he had submitted when commanded to treat Him as any other man. The crowds that gathered around Him could throng about Him in the streets; yet even they were filled with wonder at His teaching, because He spoke with authority and not as the scribes and Pharisees. His apostles could be still more familiar with Him, eating with Him, lying down beside Him to sleep, yet even they wondered, saying: 'What manner of man is this, for he commandeth the winds and the water, and they obey him'. Men who wished to ignore Him, who had bought their farms and married wives and therefore could not come, passed Him by; yet even they were compelled to look back and say: 'The Christ when he cometh will he do more miracles than this man doeth?' His enemies, in Jerusalem and in Galilee, might declare Him an impostor, a sinner, a Samaritan, an agent of Beelzebub, the prince of devils; yet none more than they had been openly defied, had been forced at every turn to confess their weakness, had been compelled to cry out in despair: ' What shall we do ? Behold all the world goes after him.' Throughout His life Jesus had indeed been always ' meek and humble of heart ' ; but His meekness had been such that already it had ' inherited the earth ', His humility such that, on it as a foundation, the kingdom of God had begun to be built. The more we study the passing of the life of Jesus across the earth, the more we see in it a thing unique: ' as the lightning cometh from the east and passeth to the west, so shall be the coming of the Son of Man '.

But if this is true of the whole of the public life of Jesus, how much more true does it appear in the last phase of all ! The Passion is about to begin ; the week of the Passion opens with a scene of asserted mastery, such as had not been witnessed before and would not be witnessed again. ' Hosanna to the Son of David ! Blessed is he that cometh in the name of the Lord ! ' is heard on every side as He rides into the city, even into the court of His Father's house ; and when enemies remonstrate, because the very children join in the salutation, His only answer is that if they were silenced the very stones about them would be made to cry out. So for the rest of that week, so long as He chose to remain among them, He remained the master of them all. Pharisees come about Him and question Him in fear, though they had issued proclamation that if He should appear in the city He should be taken prisoner. ' Master ', they say, ' we know that thou art a true speaker, and carest not for any man ; for thou regardest not the person of men, but teachest the way of God in truth.' They spoke hypocritically ; their only aim was ' that they should catch him in his speech ' ; yet was it a confession in spite of themselves, made before all that were gathering there for the Pasch. The Sadducees followed them, and they met with no better fate: ' And the multitudes hearing were in admiration of his doctrine.' He closed those days of triumph, first so that ' no man after that durst ask him any question ', next with that solemn condemnation of them all which opens with the claim: ' Be not you called Rabbi. For one is your Master, and all you are brethren.

. . Neither be ye called masters: for one is your Master, Christ.'

He left the city unmolested, though His last words foretold: 'Behold your house shall be left to you desolate' He strode across the valley as if He were its Lord ; and when His disciples would point out to Him the beauty of the scene in the setting sun, again He spoke with authority: 'Do you see these things ? Amen, I say to you, there shall not be left here a stone upon a stone, that shall not be destroyed'. He sat down with them on the mountain-side ; before He would submit to the doom of the next few days, He would tell them of the signs of the coming of the Son of man. 'And when the Son of man shall come in his majesty, and all the angels with him, then shall he sit upon the seat of his majesty. And all nations shall be gathered together before him: and he shall separate them one from another, as the shepherd separateth the sheep from the goats. .   Then shall the king '—mark the title, for it has not been used before— ' Then shall the king say to them that shall be on his right hand: Come ye blessed of my Father, possess you the kingdom prepared for you from the foundation of the world.'

The Passion begins, but, with all the humiliation, Jesus Christ remains throughout always the Master. By His own command the place is chosen where the Supper shall be held ; when He washes the feet of His disciples, nevertheless: 'You call me Master and Lord. And you say well: for so I am. If then I, being your Lord and Master, have washed your feet, you ought also to wash one another's feet.' Even Judas, cannot go to his work until he has received permission: 'And Jesus said to him: What thou doest, do quickly. .   He therefore, having received the morsel, went out immediately. And it was night.' The rest of that Supper was all victory ; the gift of the Holy Eucharist, which should be renewed through all time ' in memory of me ' ; the foretelling of the failure of the Twelve, who, nevertheless would soon come back and all would yet be well ; the denial of Peter, who still would be converted, and would then confirm his brethren. He must needs go, but He would come back to them ; they believed in God, let them believe in Him. He must needs go, for if He went not the Paraclete would not come to them ; He would go and would send Him to them. He must needs go, that He might prepare a place for them in the kingdom, in His Father's house, where there were many mansions. He was the vine, they the branches; let them but abide in Him and all would be well. The world would hate them, but let them have courage; He had overcome the world. Let them ask for what they would in His name, and He would give it to them; hitherto they had asked for nothing in His name, let them ask and they would receive that their joy might be full. The evening closed with a claim worthy of the Master of men; it begins:

'Father, the hour is come. Glorify thy Son, that thy Son may glorify thee. As thou hast given him power over all flesh, that he may give eternal life to all thou hast given to him.' We read next that Jesus was sorrowful even unto death; that He was sad, that He was broken; that He cried to His Father, if it were possible, that the chalice might pass from Him; nevertheless, when the traitor came, Jesus had already told His captors: 'I am he', and they had fallen before Him to the ground. When they seized Him, it was not till He had given them leave: 'This is your hour and the power of darkness'. They brought Him before Annas, but Annas had no authority, and to him Jesus answered not a word. They took Him to Caiaphas, the lawful high priest, and to him when commanded He spoke; yet was it with a dignity greater than He had ever shown before: 'Thou hast said that I am (the Christ the Son of the living God). Nevertheless I say to you, hereafter you shall see the Son of man, sitting on the right hand of the power of God, and coming in the clouds of heaven.'

They brought Him next morning to the Roman governor, Pilate, the representative of the monarch of the world. Here more than ever the dignity of Jesus shines forth, as if He and not Pilate were the judge; in the way He questions him about his evidence: 'Sayest thou this thing of thyself, or have others told it thee of me?', in the way He asserts His kingship: 'Thou sayest that I am a king. For this was I born, and for this I came into the world, that I might give testimony to the truth'; in the way He describes that kingdom: 'My kingdom is not of this world. If my kingdom were of this world, my servants would certainly strive that I should not be delivered to the Jews; but now my kingdom is not from

hence ' Pilate threatened Him, but Jesus was not to be
threatened: 'Speakest thou not to me ? Knowest thou
not that I have power to crucify thee, and I have power
to release thee ? Jesus answered: Thou shouldst not
have any power against me, unless it were given thee from
above.'

Pilate knew very well which of the two was the master
and which the judge. Therefore he 'feared the more',
therefore he did what he could to win his Prisoner's release, therefore, even to the end, he persisted in calling
Him 'King'. 'What accusation do you bring against
this man ?' he had asked at the beginning, but at the
end: 'Shall I crucify your king ?' 'I find no fault in
this man', he had said after the first trial, but after the
last: 'This is Jesus of Nazareth, the King of the Jews'.
Herod had failed to subdue this Master who had formerly
defied him; the soldiers who scourged Him had something more than mockery to spur them on when they
hailed Him: 'King of the Jews'. The executioners might
hurry Him to death; but, when He chose, He made
them pause while He comforted mourners on the road-
side. He had no word of rebuke for those who injured
Him, but He had words for the 'Daughters of Jerusalem'
And it was the same on the cross. We need not repeat the
story; He was Master of the Pharisees that taunted Him,
Master of the penitent by His side, Master of the
mourners beneath Him, Master of Himself as He surrendered His life to His Father, Master of those looking
on who concluded the story with the confession: 'Indeed,
this was the Son of God'.

Nor need we dwell on the days after He was dead and
buried and rose again; the mastery then goes without
saying. That His tomb should have been so carefully
guarded, even if it were by those who did not believe,
speaks volumes for the power His very remembrance
wielded over His enemies. That women should come in
the morning twilight to do His dead body honour proves
His influence upon the most timid of His own. Peter and
John hear strange things about the tomb, and they are
drawn to it as to a magnet. Mary Magdalen loses Him,
and she will do all manner of superhuman things, if only
they will tell her where His body lies. Men wander off
to their homes not knowing what to make of this paradox
'concerning Jesus of Nazareth, who was a prophet, mighty

in work and word before God and all the people'; who 'was to have redeemed Israel', yet now was dead. Other things they might doubt; of the majesty of Jesus they had no doubt whatsoever. A disciple said he did not believe; Jesus stood before him, submissive yet commanding, and he could only fall down before Him saying: 'My Lord and my God!' He stood by the lakeside where seven men were fishing; He invited them to breakfast: 'And none of them who were at meat durst ask him: Who art thou? Knowing that it was the Lord.' He gathered them about Him for the last time and gave them His final commission; it was given in the language of the Master of the world:

'All power is given to me in heaven and in earth. Going therefore, teach ye all nations: baptising them in the name of the Father and of the Son and of the Holy Ghost. Teaching them to observe all things whatsoever I have commanded you. And behold I am with you all days, even to the consummation of the world.'

It is well to emphasise the fact of the consistent majesty of Jesus, from the first moment when the angels proclaim Him to the moment when they came again and received His body out of the sight of men. That He grew in self-consciousness, that He discovered Himself in any way, there is not a shadow of evidence; from the first He was, and He knew that He was, the Master of men, their Way, their Truth, and their Life. There is never any increase in the authority He claimed and with which He acted; 'He commanded', is said of Him many times, early and late in His career, and always He was obeyed, as if nothing else could be done. 'I must be about my Father's business.' 'I say to thee, arise, take up thy bed and walk.' 'I say to you, love your enemies.' 'I am the door of the sheepfold.' 'I am the light of the world.' 'Behold I cast out devils and do cures, to-day and to-morrow, and the third day I am consummated.' 'I have power to lay down my life and to take it up again.' 'Amen, amen I say to you.' 'Thou sayest that I am the Son of God.' 'Thou sayest that I am a king.' 'All power is given to me in heaven and in earth. Go ye therefore.' The character is the same throughout, steady, unwavering, true; He has been lifted up among men, and He has drawn all things to Himself throughout the ages.

IX

JESUS AND THE LAWYERS

IN the tenth chapter of St. Luke's Gospel we read that while Our Lord was speaking to the people, ' a certain Pharisee prayed him that he would dine with him '. Jesus accepted the invitation ; but during the dinner something occurred which gave Him occasion to upbraid this class for their teaching and the manner of their lives. Then St. Luke goes on: ' And one of the lawyers answering saith to him: Master, in saying these things, thou reproachest us also.

' But he said: Woe to you lawyers also, because you load men with burdens which they cannot bear, and you yourselves touch not the packs with one of your fingers. Woe to you who build the monuments of the prophets: and your fathers killed them. Truly you bear witness that you consent to the doings of your fathers. For they indeed killed them: and you build their sepulchres. For this cause also the wisdom of God said: I will send to them prophets and apostles ; and some of them they will kill and persecute. That the blood of all the prophets which was shed from the foundation of the world may be required of this generation ; from the blood of Abel unto the blood of Zacharias, who was slain between the altar and the temple. Yea, I say to you: It shall be required of this generation. Woe to you, lawyers, for you have taken away the key of knowledge. You yourselves have not entered in: and those that were entering in, you have hindered ' (xi, 45-52).

Whereupon, when He had made this charge, we are told:

' As he was saying these things to them, the Pharisees and the lawyers began violently to urge him and to oppress his mouth about many things, lying in wait for him, and seeking to catch something from his mouth, that they might accuse him ' (xi, 53, 54).

From this passage three things seem clear: first, that the lawyers of Jerusalem did not look upon themselves as in quite the same category as the Pharisees ; second, that nevertheless Christ Our Lord had much the same charges to make against them ; third, from the concluding sentence we are shown that the unscrupulous lawyer in those days was not very different from, and used much the same means as, the unscrupulous lawyer in every other generation ; they 'lay in wait for him ; seeking to catch something from his mouth, that they might accuse him '.

Who were these 'lawyers', and what was the specific charge which Our Lord had to make against them ? That He did not condemn all law as such is clear. No man was ever more careful about the observance of the Law ; even when, later, He spoke more violently still against the Pharisees and lawyers, He nevertheless insisted that they were to be obeyed:

'The scribes and Pharisees have sitten on the chair of Moses. All things, therefore, whatsoever they shall say to you, observe and do, but according to their works do ye not. For they say, and do not ' (Matt. xxiii, 2, 3).

Manifestly, therefore, it was against a special type of lawyer that He inveighed, and He inveighed against them, not because of their office, for He acknowledged that they 'sat upon the chair of Moses' and were therefore to be obeyed, but because of the use they made of it.

We need not delay to show, what seems universally accepted by Scripture scholars, that the terms 'lawyer', 'scribe', and 'doctor of the law' mean the same thing in the Gospels. The Law of Moses, as found in the Pentateuch, was the material out of which the whole of Jewish life was built ; long before the birth of Our Lord its express written code, and the oral interpretation which accompanied it, had become the fixed guide, not in religious and moral matters only, but in every detail of a Jew's ordinary day. It will be obvious at once that the average Jew could not interpret the Law to such an extent for himself. For, first, it was written in a language which few Jews in the time of Our Lord could understand ; their language at that period was Aramaic, and the Law was written in the ancient Hebrew. Secondly, the Law as it stood did not include every-day events ; it had been adapted to these in the course of centuries by successive interpretations, and these interpretations were more or less codified in books which were in the hands of a select class or caste. Still every faithful Jew believed that his fidelity in the eyes of God depended on his fidelity to the word of God as he had learnt to accept it, to the Law. Hence it became absolutely necessary that there should arise a special class, a profession if you like, of men who would make the Law from this point of view a special study. It would be their task to collect, study, and expound the traditional interpretation of the Law, the ' traditions of the fathers ', as it was called ; to apply that interpretation to cases of ordinary life as they occurred ; to find, if they could, some precedent for every decision or ruling ; to frame new regulations that would be in keeping with what had gone before. In other words, they were men whose whole occupation was to define what was legal, and what was illegal, down to the smallest details of life ; gradually this had reached so far that there was scarcely an action of the day, from morning to night, which was not regulated by the Law, and the traditions which had gathered round it.

These students and interpreters were the ' lawyers ', the ' scribes ', the ' doctors of the law '. Naturally they were men of great authority. Though officially they had no special standing, still it almost followed of necessity that the judges of the country were taken from their ranks ; though they were in no sense priests, still their greater knowledge, both of the Scriptures and of the Jewish practice, made them usually the chief speakers in all religious meetings. Moreover, as the third of their names implies, the teaching of the Law was almost entirely in their hands. In the time of Our Lord there were special schools for the study of the Law, most of all in Jerusalem ; it was in one of these that Our Lord was found, after He had been lost by His parents at the age of twelve :

' They found him in the Temple, sitting in the midst of the doctors, hearing them and asking them questions ' (Luke ii, 46).

Authority such as this, in the law courts, in religious casuistry, in the schools, laid the lawyer open to a great temptation to indulge in arrogance and pride. There was little or no appeal against him ; he held, as it were, all the strings in his own hands ; gradually he received the most extravagant honour, both from his pupils and from ordinary men. According to the Talmud he was to be reverenced more than a father, and he had come to look for this external recognition as belonging to his office. It was this which Our Lord specially attacked in a short address:

' Beware of the scribes, who love to walk in long robes, and to be saluted in the market-place: and to sit in the first chairs in the synagogues and to have the highest places at suppers: who devour the houses of widows under the pretence of long prayer. These shall receive greater judgement' (Mark xii, 38-40).

It is not to be supposed either that this was the state of all the lawyer caste in the time of Our Lord, or that it had been so all through the years preceding. Esdras, the restorer of the Jews to Jerusalem after the Babylonian Captivity, is described, or more probably describes himself, as ' a ready scribe in the Law of Moses which the Lord had given to Israel' (I Esdras vii, 6). In the *Book of Ecclesiasticus* there is a long and beautiful passage, depicting the ideal scribe ; a passage which indicates the esteem in which the scribe, or lawyer, was rightly held by the observant Jew, both before the coming of Our Lord and during His time. Nor must it be supposed that because He inveighed against them in general, therefore there were not some who were true to their calling ; there were faithful and truth-seeking Pharisees, like Nicodemus, there were faithful scribes, like Gamaliel. Nevertheless, the main body had been hardened, and their influence had perverted the whole practice and teaching of the Law. Here it is well to notice that it was not Jesus who first attacked them, but they who first attacked Him. From the beginning of His public life to the end, the Pharisees and scribes opposed Him ; knowing very well that not only His teaching but His whole attitude to religion was contrary to theirs. He associated with publicans and sinners, whom they had ruled out of recognition ; He was indifferent to certain ceremonial practices, which they had declared to be essential to the service of God ; He disregarded their injunctions concerning the Sabbath, declaring that the Sabbath was made for man, and not man for the Sabbath. In consequence, in order to put Him in the wrong, they would set Him leading questions, asking Him the way of entering into eternal life ; which was the greatest of the commandments ; whether or not divorce was lawful ; whether it were lawful to pay tribute to a foreign power ; whether a woman convicted of sin should, as the Law dictated, be stoned to death.

From all this it is clear that the scribes and Pharisees recognised Our Lord from first to last as an enemy ; when at the beginning they asked Him 'by what authority' He acted, when later they 'asked Him for a sign', when again they did all they could to belittle Him in the eyes of the people—'A prophet cometh not out of Galilee'—we have it clearly stated that they saw in Him an enemy to the whole foundation of their doctrine, and even of their very thrones. Consequently, when He turned upon them, and heaped upon them insulting names, hypocrites, whited sepulchres, offspring of vipers and serpents, an evil and adulterous generation, blind guides, whose leaven above all things was to be avoided, and who, with all their show of righteousness, would find publicans and harlots entering heaven before themselves, we do not find them taken by surprise, we scarcely find them indignant or insulted ; we only hear that they were the more determined to do Him to death, and for this purpose were willing to ally themselves even with their own bitterest rivals.

What, then, was the reason why Jesus, who revered the Law, who, as He said of Himself, had 'come not to destroy the Law but to perfect it', was so strongly opposed to these masters of the Law, whom, nevertheless, He commanded His followers to obey ? We may sum up the whole matter in a single phrase which a scholar has framed ; while none more than Christ was obedient to the Law, yet none more than He resisted 'the idolatry and tyranny of the Law'. The Law, argued the lawyers, was God's own gift to Israel, and to Israel alone ; it was the one thing that separated them from the rest of the world, made them a 'holy' people as distinguished from all others. The Law, moreover, as God had delivered it, was the one sure means of salvation, both for the people of the Jews, and for each individual Jew that composed it ; a faithful Jew need do nothing more in his life than study and carry out the Law, and he would be a perfect man in the eyes of God. From this rigid principle, however much truth lay beneath it, there had grown up the belief, which had become a recognised convention, that religion, relation with God, was mainly an external affair, the fulfilment of certain obligations which God had imposed. God was no longer the Shepherd, the Forgiving Father, so often dwelt on in the Psalms, or appealed to in the Prophets ; He was the Lawgiver, He was the Judge, whose commands were to be obeyed to the letter, whose judgement was to be feared above all else. There was deep significance in the answer of Our Lord, when asked which was the first commandment of the Law. He laid aside all allusion to ceremonial, even all allusion to the Decalogue, though on another occasion He said that their observance would suffice. Instead, since it was a lawyer who asked Him, He said at once: ' The first commandment is this, Thou shalt love the Lord thy God '.

On this foundation much had been built. Since religion was no more than the fulfilment of a law, a purely legal compact, and in no sense a fellowship, a life with God, it almost followed that holiness consisted in a strict observance of the Law ; the more a man brought it into his life, applying it if possible to every detail, the greater ' saint ' he might be thought to be. And since this was mainly an external matter, it almost followed likewise that this external holiness should be seen by the eyes of men ; a man was ' holy ' who was observed by others to be in all things a strict keeper of the Law. Thus the Law, as it were, was not only deified, made the absolute and final norm of all things temporal and spiritual ; it was also enlarged and expanded to an extravagant extent. Precepts were multiplied to meet all manner of special cases, fresh laws were added, to ensure that the original law should be more properly observed ; the Law was hedged in on all sides, to secure that its violation should be impossible. The more zealous Jews, those who ambitioned repute for holiness, would not be content with what the Law commanded ; they would anticipate the command, they would add laws for themselves which would seem to be in the spirit of the former ; in their keeping of the Law they considered less the spirit that was behind it, more its actual words, and whether it was fulfilled or not in any particular action.

The application of this to their actual lives may best be seen from the detailed charges made against them by Our Lord, which charges, as such, they never denied, however much they resented the interpretation put upon them. They fasted ' that they might be seen by men to fast ' ;

they prayed in the open, in such a way that others might behold them ; they made much of food, of meats clean and unclean, of washings before eating, and of similar practices of external cleanliness, as if they sufficed for the washing of the whole man ; as someone has said, 'they made the Law a manual of religious etiquette.' And this led to many other evils ; above all to a false estimate of what was right and what was wrong. They divorced morality from religion ; they put the offering of sacrifice before the doing of an act of mercy, dutiful fulfilment of a ceremony before duty to one's own parents, going to the altar before the forgiveness of injuries and reconciliation even with one's own brother, the observance of the Sabbath before an act of charity, however pressing. Lastly, under such a covering, when right and wrong had been so confounded, it was no surprise that they should be interchanged ; right became wrong, and wrong became right, and because of the initial assumptions this was not noticed. It was not thought strange that he who was so devoted to the observance of the Law should be rewarded with the good things of this world ; in the service of the Temple scribes and Pharisees grew rich. It was right that they should be honoured for their sanctity by their fellow-men ; they paraded before them, and were paid reverence wherever they went. Being the representatives of the voice of God, it was becoming that they should enact new laws in His name ; and since His Laws restricted, theirs should restrict and bind still more.

It was against such an attitude as this that Christ Our Lord primarily inveighed, and on such a background that His strong words should be studied. God was indeed the Source of all things, the Lord and Master, the Maker of the Law, and the Judge before whom all observance or non-observance of the Law should be judged. But more than all this He was the Father, and it is as such that Jesus always describes Him, whether He speaks of His own relation to Him, or of God's relation to men. He Himself came into the world to be 'about His Father's business ' ; when His life was over He summed it up in the words: ' Father, I have finished the work thou gavest me to do.' And in exactly the same terms He spoke of obedience ; religion was not merely a fulfilment of a law, it was sonship of the Father, and therefore obedience to the Father, founded on the trust and heartfelt love of a son. It was not, primarily, a question of merit, or of being rewarded for service ; it was the willing, and even proud fulfilment of the will of One who loves, and whom man loves in return. The love of God, and the love of man which necessarily flowed from it, that, said Our Lord, was 'the Law and the prophets' ; St. Paul later, interpreting his Master, says that in this is included all the Law.

Hence, with this principle laid down, Christ Our Lord does not hesitate to descend to detail. He contrasts the consequences: 'You have heard that it hath been said: Thou shalt love thy neighbour and hate thy enemy. But I say to you: Love your enemies: do good to them that hate you: and pray for them that persecute and calumniate you: that you may be the children of your Father who is in heaven, who maketh his sun to rise upon the good and bad, and raineth upon the just and the unjust' (Matthew v, 43-45).

He emphasises that true religion is not mere outward fulfilment of a code, but an inner moral life of which the outward practice is a sign.

'You make clean the outside of the cup and of the platter: but inside you are full of rapine and iniquity. Ye fools, did not he that made that which is without make also that which is within ? ' (Luke xi, 39, 40).

He insists that the defilement of a man is not merely soiling which can be washed away with water, but the evil that is in his heart:

'For from within, out of the heart of men, proceed evil thoughts, adulteries, fornications, murders, thefts, covetousness, wickedness, deceit, lasciviousness, an evil eye, blasphemy, pride, foolishness. All these evil things come from within and defile a man' (Mark vii, 21-23).

No action, He repeats, not even a good action of which the scribes and their allies made so much, was of any real worth unless it expressed the dispositions of the inner man.

Not alms-giving: 'When thou givest alms, let not thy left hand know what thy right hand doth: that thy alms may be in secret, and thy Father, who seeth in secret, will repay thee' (Matthew vi, 3, 4).

Not prayer:

'When thou shalt pray, enter into thy chamber, and having shut the door, pray to thy Father in secret: and thy Father, who seeth in secret, will repay thee ' (Matthew vi, 6).

Not fasting:

' And when you fast, be not as the hypocrites, sad. For they disfigure their faces, that they may appear unto men to fast. Amen I say to you, they have received their reward. But thou, when thou dost fast, anoint thy head and wash thy face: that thou appear not to men to fast, but to thy Father who is in secret. And thy Father, who seeth in secret, will repay thee ' (Matthew vi, 16-18).

We may now sum up the attitude of Christ Our Lord, both to the Law and to the Jewish lawyers. A Jew Himself, He was, as St. Paul says, ' born under the law ' (Gal. iv, 4). As boy and man He submitted to its requirements, to circumcision, to presentation in the Temple as a firstborn, to be made, at twelve years of age, a ' son of the Law '. Again and again, when the time of His public life began, He recognised the Law to be a Divine institution, and He spoke of its authority with the strongest approval. The Law was, to Him, God's law ; it came from God, and was God's revelation ; He had come ' not to destroy the Law or the prophets ; not to destroy but to fulfil ' (Matthew v, 17). Again and again, moreover, He appeals to Moses and the Law in His own defence, and in confirmation of His own teaching. One man is told: ' If thou wouldst enter into life, keep the commandments ' (Matthew xix, 17) and no more. Another asks: ' What shall I do to gain eternal life ? ' and the answer is given: ' What is written in the Law ? ' (Luke x, 26). We have seen already how carefully He bade His hearers obey those who sat on the chair of Moses, even while He was pronouncing upon them scathing condemnation for the way they had annulled the Law by word and deed.

Nevertheless, Jesus took it upon Himself to criticise, not only the lawyers, but even the Law itself. He said that ' the Law and the prophets were until John ' (Luke xvi, 16), expressly intimating that then it ceased in its full authority, and that a new era had begun. He took point after point of the teaching of the Law, and deliberately with an ' I say to you ' to introduce each clause, He laid down a new standard of life for all to follow. Indeed, He laid aside all legalism, and substituted in its place ideals the most sublime. Likeness to Himself, love like to His love, the example of the Father who is in heaven, the fulfilment of the will of that Father, these are to be Law enough for the future ; and these are the 'fulfilment' of that Old Law which hitherto had been enough, but whose spirit had been killed through too close attention to the letter. The time had come for the new order ; the greater prophet whom Moses had foretold had appeared :

'The Lord thy God will raise up to thee a Prophet of thy nation and of thy brethren, like unto me. Him thou shalt hear' (Deuteronomy xviii, 15).

But this was, in matter of fact, an entirely different question from that which we have been considering. Jesus was no enemy of the Law ; it was in its defence, not in its condemnation, that He opposed the scribes and the Pharisees ; He appealed to Moses against them, saying that if they had only interpreted Moses rightly they would easily have discovered Himself. He pointed out to them that, in their excessive legalism, in their attention to the rigid letter, they had forgotten the first commandment of the Law itself ; and once, when a lawyer confessed that He was right, that the love of God was the first law of all, He promptly said to him: 'Thou art not far from the kingdom of God.' They had made the Law, not a way to God, but a substitution for going along that way ; not a means to an end, but an end in itself. There was something more than the Law as they interpreted it ; there was love, and the higher Law which the service of love entailed. Obedience to Law alone led to slavery ; obedience directed by love was liberty, of which Our Lord spoke when He told His disciples that 'the truth would make them free'

The contest is one that has often been repeated through history. Leave out love, and there is nothing but the iron hand of man-made Law that can keep the world in order. Bring in love, love of God and love of men, and there is little need for Law. For championing this principle Christ Our Lord was put to death, and many a man has died for the same cause. Sir Thomas More was convicted of high treason ; he, too, had refused to obey the Law ; but in his life and in his death he showed that he obeyed a higher Law, and he died as his Master had died, interpreting as a master of the Law himself the right relation between the law of men and the law of God, the law of human convention and the law that comes from the love of the Father who is in heaven.

X

HAVING COMPASSION

THERE is one word recurring in the Gospels which seems to give us more insight than any other into the character of Our Lord Jesus Christ. It is the word which is translated 'having compassion', but in fact its meaning goes very much deeper down than our English word, and might perhaps be better rendered 'being touched to the heart'. It occurs in the Gospels twelve times, and on each occasion gives us a flash of light on the human side of Jesus which leaves a complete impression.

The first occasion is very early in His life. He had gone away from Capharnaum on His first tour of preaching through Galilee. In the midst of His preaching, apparently in a village where He is alone, a leper appeals to Him:

And there came a leper to him
Beseeching him
And kneeling down said to him
If thou wilt
Thou canst make me clean
And Jesus having compassion on him
(Touched to the heart at sight of him)
Stretching forth his hand
And touching him, saith to him
I will
Be thou made clean
And when he had spoken
Immediately the leprosy departed from him
And he was made clean.

Mark i, 40-42.

The story is told by Matthew, Mark, and Luke, and by all with the same simplicity. There are no conditions laid down; there is no other motive given but Our Lord's intense human sympathy for human suffering; even after it is over the healed man is asked to say nothing about it. It would seem to be just a spontaneous act of Jesus and no more, and as such the Evangelists seem to describe it.

The second occasion is outside the gate of the walled city of Naim. The story is well known. It is still comparatively early in His life; the Twelve have been chosen, the Sermon on the Mount has been preached.

> And it came to pass afterwards
> That he went into a city that is called Naim
> And there went with him his disciples
> And a great multitude
> And when he came nigh to the gate of the city
> Behold a dead man was carried out
> The only son of his mother
> And she was a widow
> And a great multitude of the city was with her
> Whom when the Lord had seen
> Being moved with mercy towards her
> (Touched to the heart at sight of her)
> He said to her: Weep not
> And he came near
> And touched the bier
> And they that carried it stood still
> And he said
> Young man
> I say to thee, arise
> And he that was dead sat up
> And began to speak
> And he gave him to his mother.
>
> Luke vii, 11-15.

Once more there are no conditions, either before or after the miracle; there is not even a request that He should do anything, it does not occur to anyone that there is anything to be done. Jesus has come across the valley in the afternoon. He has met a funeral procession, the chief mourner in which is a widow; and human sympathy for human suffering seems to get the better of His human heart. The last words show His motive; He works this greatest of His miracles so far recorded, and immediately passes on.

The third occasion occurs towards the end of His life.

He is on the way up from Jericho to Jerusalem, a day or two before the first Palm Sunday.

> And when they went out from Jericho
> A great multitude followed him
> And behold two blind men sitting by the wayside
> Heard that Jesus passed by
> And they cried out saying
> O Lord, thou Son of David
> Have mercy on us
> And the multitude rebuked them
> That they should hold their peace
> But they cried out the more saying
> O Lord, thou Son of David
> Have mercy on us
> And Jesus stood and called them
> And said: What will ye that I do to you?
> They say to him
> Lord, that our eyes may be opened
> And Jesus having compassion on them
> (Touched to the heart at sight of them)
> Touched their eyes
> And immediately they saw
> And followed him.
>
> Matthew xx, 29-34.

It is the same here as before. The only motive given for the miracle is the human sympathy of the human heart of Jesus, making it long to relieve human suffering. No conditions are laid down; on each occasion the healing hand is stretched out, touching the leper, touching the dead man's bier, touching the eyes of the two blind beggars, let the consequences be what they may.

On one occasion only do we find the word in the mouth of another. It is after the Transfiguration. When Jesus came down from the mountain along with the three apostles, they found the other disciples at the foot with a wild demoniac in their midst. They had tried to deliver him and had failed, and were being held up to shame in consequence. Jesus came near and the crowd appealed to Him, especially the father of the mad child pleaded piteously.

> And he asked his father
> How long is it since this hath happened to him?

But he said
From his infancy
And oftentimes hath he cast him into the fire
And into waters to destroy him
But if thou canst do anything
Help us
Having compassion on us
(Touched to the heart at sight of us.)

Mark ix, 20-21.

The last argument prevailed. Jesus had blamed the people for their want of faith. He had blamed even the father. But in return the father had touched the tender spot in the heart of Jesus, and the issue was secure.

These are the only places where the word is used by the Evangelists as it were instinctively, in their description of Our Lord's dealing with individual suffering. But still more remarkable are the instances of its use when Jesus stands before a crowd ; the sight of a crowd would seem to have moved Him to sympathy even more than the sight of individual suffering.

The first instance occurs in one of those general summaries, not uncommon in the Gospel of St. Matthew.

And Jesus went about all the cities and towns
Teaching in their synagogues
And preaching the Gospel of the Kingdom
And healing every disease and every infirmity
And seeing the multitudes
He had compassion on them
(He was touched to the heart at sight of them)
Because they were distressed
And lying like sheep that have no shepherd
Then he saith to his disciples
The harvest indeed is great
But the labourers are few
Pray ye therefore the Lord of the Harvest
That he send forth labourers into his harvest.

Matthew ix, 35-38.

It is easy to be 'touched to the heart' at the sight of an individual in actual suffering ; not so easy to feel the agony and distress that usually lies within and beneath the gathering of a motley crowd. Yet here the Evangelist clings to the same word for his description ; he can find no better. Jesus looked on the multitude that came after Him ; others might have been stirred by its enthusiasm, He was only distressed. He saw the individual members that made it up, confused by the guides that should have led them, willing to be led if the right leader would appear, not knowing their own loss, the aimlessness of their lives. He felt for them more than they knew, more than they felt for themselves ; what might not be made of men, anywhere, at any time, if only the right leaders led them ! A crowd can do cruel things which an individual man will not do ; yet it is not the crowd that is most guilty.

In another place St. Mark makes use of the same expression. It is before the miracle of the Feeding of the Five Thousand. The apostles had returned from their first missionary expedition, and Jesus had taken them away to give them a rest from their labours. But the people had discovered their departure, and had gone round the lake after Him. Then we are told:

> And Jesus going out
> Saw a great multitude
> And he had compassion on them
> (He was touched to the heart at sight of them)
> Because they were as sheep not having a shepherd
> And he began to teach them many things.
>
> Mark vi, 34.

The repetition of the phrase makes us realise that it was not St. Mark's own, nor St. Matthew's own ; it had come from some other source, and what other source could there have been but that of Jesus Himself ? He was the Good Shepherd, and He knew His own. Other sheep there were that were not of His fold, and them also must He bring to Himself ; He had been sent for the lost sheep of the house of Israel. Therefore when He looked upon the helpless crowd, probably not once but many times He would speak of them as sheep without a shepherd ; and never more than when in their helplessness they came to Him not knowing what they did. Poor human nature ! It was indeed badly off ; of itself it could do nothing. Yet it knew no better ; and it went to the heart of Jesus Christ that it should be so distraught, ignorant though it was of its plight. So He gave up His day of rest, and made the apostles give up theirs. He surrendered Himself once more to a day of labour and teaching.

In the account of the same scene St. Matthew again uses the word, regardless of the fact that he has used it before.

> And he coming forth
> Saw a great multitude
> And had compassion on them
> (Was touched to the heart at sight of them)
> And healed their sick.
>
> Matthew xiv, 14.

Once more it is the same motive that urges Him ; not only, as in St. Mark, to spend the day in teaching them, but to move about among them, and in other ways to make them happy. He does not discriminate ; His miracles do not appear to be reserved for those who profess faith in Him ; even though He knows that many come for the miracles and nothing else, yet He does not, so far, stay His hand. He is ' touched to the heart at sight of them ', and apparently that is enough. Whatever may come after He must stoop down to comfort them, and to make their sick sound and well.

The last occasion is when for the second time He feeds the multitude in the desert. The Evangelists, St. Mark in particular, have gone out of their way to make it quite clear that Jesus performed this miracle twice ; it would almost seem that he foresaw that men would endeavour to confound the two, and that he wished to anticipate the objection. The places are different ; the circumstances are different ; the crowds for whom the miracles are performed are altogether different in their composition ; the effect in each case was such as suited the different gatherings, and was by no means the same. On the first occasion when five thousand were fed, it was done for a multitude of Jews, from Capharnaum and its neighbourhood, who had followed Him round the northern shore of the lake of Galilee ; the second time when He fed four thousand it was for a mixed congregation of Jews and Gentiles, perhaps chiefly Gentiles, who had come to Him out of Decapolis and had been with Him three days. In the former scene Jesus is said to have ' had compassion ', because the multitude were ' as sheep without a shepherd ',

in the second there is no mention of this, His compassion
is attributed to quite another cause.

The story is told by both St. Matthew and St. Mark, in
very similar terms, but especially at the beginning do
the authors speak alike. Thus St. Mark:

> In those days
> Again when there was a great multitude
> And they had nothing to eat
> Calling his disciples together
> He said to them
> I have compassion on the multitude
> (I am touched to the heart at sight of the multitude)
> For behold they have been with me three days
> And have nothing to eat
> And if I shall send them away fasting to their homes
> They will faint in the way.
>
> Mark viii, 1-3.

And St. Matthew:

> And Jesus called together his disciples and said
> I have compassion on the multitude
> (I am touched to the heart at sight of the multitude)
> Because they continue with me now three days
> And have not what to eat
> And I will not send them away fasting
> Lest they faint in the way.
>
> Matthew xv, 32.

In this second multiplication one may say the compassion of Jesus was even more 'human' than before.
He had already, as on the former occasion, 'taught them
many things', He had already healed their sick; one
might have supposed that He had shown these comparative strangers compassion enough. But no; His human
heart was touched by the mere human privation of this
multitude of men, women, and children, and He must do
what human kindness prompted Him to do.

There remain three other places where the word occurs
in the Gospels; in each of these places it is used, and very
significantly, by Our Lord Himself.

The first is in the Parable of the Good Samaritan. A
poor man lay robbed and wounded by the road-side. A
priest passed by and took no notice, a Levite did likewise; but at length

A certain Samaritan
Being on his journey came near him
And seeing him was moved with compassion
(Was touched to the heart)
And going up to him bound up his wounds
Pouring in oil and wine
And setting him upon his own beast
Brought him to an inn
And took care of him.

Luke x, 33, 34.

Now from the story of the Good Samaritan it is usual to draw the lesson which the man drew to whom it was first told: the lesson, that is, of 'showing mercy'. Even if Jesus wins so much and no more from one, who, in the strict sense, at all events, is no follower, He is content; many an unbeliever will be saved simply because he has 'shown mercy' to his neighbour. Nevertheless, in matter of fact, the parable contains much more than this; the very build of the story shows it. The chief sentence of the passage is not that which tells of the Samaritan's kind actions. The deliberate climax of the drama is contained in the words:

Seeing him was moved with compassion
(Was touched to the heart.)

All the rest only follows as a natural consequence. In other words, though 'mercy' is approved as one fruit of the story, the real fruit is 'compassion', being touched to the heart, from which real mercy must flow. It must be remembered that the parable is given to illustrate the commandment: 'Thou shalt love thy neighbour as thyself', not merely 'Thou shalt show mercy to him' and if, as is common, the Good Samaritan is found impersonated in Our Lord Jesus Christ Himself, then we may say, from His own description of the best He saw in another, that 'having compassion' had the first place in His own heart. 'Out of the abundance of the heart the mouth speaketh.'

The second passage is in the parable of the Prodigal Son. The poor, deluded youth had gone off with his money; he had had a 'good time' according to his own idea, and the 'good time' had ended, as it often ends, in a pigsty. Penitent and ragged he was tramping home, hardly daring to hope for forgiveness, yet counting on his father's mercy. Then Jesus adds, in the light of what has been already said, revealing His own nature in every word:

> And when he was yet a great way off
> His father saw him
> And was moved with compassion
> (Was touched to the heart)
> And running to him
> Fell upon his neck
> And kissed him.
>
> Luke xv, 20.

In other words here He goes yet further; not only is compassion His own characteristic, it is the characteristic of the Father, His Father and ours. Once more it is the turning point of the whole story, the rest follows as an obvious sequel, manifesting the joy of the Father while the Prodigal Son almost disappears from view.

The same is repeated quite needlessly, yet quite naturally, in another parable. Here it is not the chief verb; it is only a parenthesis. At first one might say that the point of the parable is secured without it; but the word seems to come to the lips of Jesus with the ease of habit, so that He must use it in this place. It is in the parable of the 'King who would take an account of his servants'. One was found hopelessly in debt, so great that no single man could hope to pay it. He was condemned to be sold; he pleaded for mercy; and the parable continues:

> And the lord of that servant
> Being moved with pity
> (Touched to the heart)
> Let him go
> And forgave him the debt.
>
> Matthew xviii, 27.

After all that has been said, this last illustration of the use of the word needs no further comment; except that the forgiveness of the debt of 'ten thousand talents', a colossal fortune, is attributed to nothing else but that the king had been 'touched to the heart'.

With these examples before us is it not safe to say that the greatest charity, as Jesus understands it, is not necessarily to do charitable acts, but so to appreciate the sufferings of others as to feel them in ourselves ? Nay, often to feel for others when they themselves are unaware that they are in need of compassion ? Given the interior grief the external acts will follow ; without it even 'charity' may, as the apostle says, be no more than a 'tinkling cymbal' and 'profit nothing'. Many years ago the writer was sitting at a window with a mother of many sons. There was great pomp and ceremony going on in the street outside. A war was being fought somewhere and troops were marching past to be embarked for the front. Bands were playing, soldiers were making merry, the crowd was lavish with flags and flowers, and every mark of joy. By chance I looked at the mother beside me. The tears were flowing down her cheeks ; when she saw I had noticed it she quietly remarked: 'Poor boys, they are somebody's children !'

Her heart had gone out to those men. It had gone deeper down than the crowd. It had passed beyond to the distant homes where fathers and mothers were weeping, and it was weeping with them. Perhaps something of this kind was what the Evangelists meant when they said, more than once, that Jesus 'was touched to the heart' at the sight of a multitude of human beings.

XI

THE WITNESS OF PONTIUS PILATE[1]

WRITERS of various schools are agreed that from the point of view of Jewish Law, the condemnation of Jesus, by Caiaphas first and by the Sanhedrin afterwards, was nothing more or less than a judicial murder. More than one have summed up the violations of the Law contained in the accounts of the trial, some Jewish authors assert that they are so many as to make the whole story impossible. The preliminary examination before Annas, the fact that no specific charge was brought against their Captive, the trial by night, expressly forbidden, the blow given by the guard, the confusion of the witnesses, the condemnation of Jesus on His own evidence alone, the fact that even this condemnation was not explicitly formulated, the contumely poured out upon Him after His guilt had been assumed, all this, and possibly much more, was contrary to the procedure of the Jewish Court. It would seem that the consciousness of this was the reason for the further trial held early on the following morning; that the 'chief priests and ancients' might be justified in bringing the case before Pilate, their own condemnation of Jesus must be legalised. Accordingly,

'As soon as it was day, straightway all the chief priests and ancients of the people and scribes came together and held a council against Jesus to put him to death.'

In other words, the high court of ecclesiastical justice held a preliminary meeting to make quite sure that, this

[1] For the most part the author does not claim any originality in this interpretation of the trial before Pilate. He knows he has read some similar account elsewhere, but he cannot recall the place. He trusts that in the present chapter he has not infringed the rights of any authors or has been guilty of flagrant plagiarism. On the other hand, the remarkable conformity of the whole account with the forms of Roman Law seems to deserve mention in this series of Witnesses. The conformity with which the story is told confirms the impression that it is the writing of a contemporary

time, there must be no disagreement. The witnesses could be dispensed with ; they had done their part overnight, however badly, since they had not been prepared. Caiaphas had given those official judges the line they could follow, with certainty of success ; they would concentrate on the Prisoner Himself. He had been asked one question, which alone He had answered, and His answer had condemned Him out of His own mouth. There was little time to spare ; if possible, they would have the whole execution carried out before the city was astir ; for they were still not without ' fear of the people ', and who knew but that some of His followers among the people might yet combine and release Him ? Therefore the official and legal trial must be swift and short.

' And they brought him into their council, saying : If thou be the Christ, tell us.'

It was a repetition of the night before, but what a confession of faith ! Two years before, their emissaries had asked the very same question of John the Baptist ; more than once, in Galilee and in Jerusalem, they had put it to Jesus when they had met Him. He had never denied as John had done ; on the other hand, He had always answered in a way that left them room to accept Him or not as they chose. But now the occasion was different : He stood before lawful judges, and they had a right to be answered. Still He would let them see that He was not deceived. Lawful judges they were, but they had no wish or intention to do Him justice. Moreover, He would warn them beforehand of the consequences of their act. They proposed to put the Son of Man to death ; the day would come when, in turn, the Son of Man would be their judge.

' And he said to them : If I shall tell you, you will not believe me, and if I shall ask you, you will not answer me nor let me go. But hereafter the Son of Man shall be sitting on the right hand of the power of God.'

The judges knew very well the meaning of His words ; as was His wont, He had referred these men, learned in the sacred books, to a well-known prophecy ; that they understood what He had said, their further question proved :

' Then said they all : Art thou then the Son of God ? '

Jesus knew they would ask Him this question. Caiaphas had asked it, and now He had deliberately led them up to it, that once more, this time before a lawful Court, He might give His testimony.

'And he said: You say that I am.'

We cannot here dwell on the mentality of the judges at this point. It is enough to know that, formally and explicitly, Jesus was condemned by His Jewish captors for His claim to be the Son of God, and for nothing else.

'Then they said: What need we any further testimony? For we ourselves have heard it from his own mouth.'

'Blasphemy' such as this had only one punishment. But the Romans had enacted that though the Jewish Courts could pass any other sentence, the sentence of death must be referred to the Romans themselves. There was no time to spare. Moreover, the more quickly they acted, the more likely they were to receive the sanction of the Roman Governor; at such a time, with the city in a ferment because of the Pasch, if they acted at once he might be glad to give them their will and have done with them, before further trouble came.

'And straightway the ancients and the scribes and the whole council, the whole multitude of them, rose up, and binding Jesus led him from Caiaphas to the Governor's hall, and brought him bound, and delivered him to Pilate the Governor.'

Pilate had decided many cases in his time, most of them with short shrift. But a case quite like this he had never had before. Usually, when the Jews had stood before his seat of judgement, they had clamoured for the release of their countryman; this time, strange to say, from the very first moment, before they had even formulated their charge, they called for their victim's blood. This alone put him on the alert. It was clear they wished to stampede him; it was clear, from the way they clamoured for the sentence to be passed, without any thought of either charge or evidence, that passion, hatred, and not justice, was behind their move. There must be trickery somewhere; he must tread very carefully from the beginning with these clever Asiatics, who were far more clever than himself. These Jews had come to him to pass sentence in accordance with the Roman Law; to guard himself against mistakes, he would have the Roman Law, with all its steps and formalities, strictly carried out. Thus, if at any point the trial failed, the accused would be accounted not guilty, the charge would go by default, and he would be freed from the necessity of passing sentence. He could dismiss the case and let the unconvicted Prisoner go.

Hence, to the disgust, and not a little to the alarm of the accusers, Pilate insisted on the regular form of trial. First must come the *nominis delatio;* the charge brought against the Prisoner must be clearly defined. Roman Law made no account of generalities. Before he would go any further, at least he would insist on this:

'Pilate therefore went out to meet them, and said: What accusation do you bring against this man ?'

He has used a definite legal term ; it was clear, therefore, from this formal legal question, that he did not mean to be overborne. In answer, in conformity with strict legal practice, a formal arraignment had to be made ; the lawyers called it *nomen deferre.* But the accusers were not at once prepared for this legal procedure. They had been accustomed to deal with a contemptuous Pilate, whose methods with Jews were summary ; they had not counted on this sudden change of front. Unprepared for this formal change, this demand for a *recognitio causæ,* they had failed to prepare a formal charge that would come within cognisance of the Roman Law ; that their Prisoner had declared Himself the Son of God could have meant nothing in a Roman court of justice. But was Pilate really in earnest ? Did he mean to institute a formal trial ? They would put him to the test ; they would try an evasion ; by a justification of themselves, on which he could act if he was so disposed, they would give him an opportunity to avoid further legal proceedings.

'They answered and said to him: If he were not a malefactor, we would not have delivered him up to thee.'

Such an answer, clearly, was no matter for instant capital punishment ; it was not even matter for the Roman Court. If this were all they would say, it was no concern of his ; if they would have him pass sentence, they must prefer a definite charge. He could refer them back to their own judges and dismiss the case.

'Pilate then said to them: Take him you, and judge him according to your law.'

He could now claim the liberty to retire, and leave these accusers to their own devices. But, of course, this was not in accordance with their minds ; they had determined on their victim's death, and only Pilate could secure it. Therefore, before any charge had yet been framed, they must let him know why they had come to him, and what they expected from him.

'The Jews therefore said to him: It is not lawful for us to put anyone to death.'

Pilate could not have been surprised by this protest. His first attempt to escape had failed, but there were others. He accepted the challenge their words implied ; he would take the matter into his own hands, go through with it step by step, according to the letter of the Law, confident that somewhere it would break down. Though the life of a Jew, and even justice to a Jew, were of little concern to him, still there were occasions when it behoved him to act like a Roman, observing strict law and order ; even a common peasant such as this man before him, since His accusers had appealed to the law, should not be put to death without at least the due legal formalities. The trial, then, must begin from the beginning. There must be a formal charge of actual crime, and a *recognitio causæ*, a formal acknowledgement by the judge that the charge preferred involved some breach of Roman Law.

By this time the accusers had been able to formulate their charge, their *accusatio*, their *criminis delatio* for which they had before been at a loss. Unable to bring their real charge, they must invent something which would bring their victim within the scope of the Roman Courts. It should consist of three counts, each of which would be most likely to impress a Roman. Now there were three things which the Imperial Authority would not tolerate, and often punished with death: sedition, refusal to pay the Imperial dues, and revolt. These three charges, then, they would bring against their Prisoner ; if to preserve the forms of justice were all that Pilate sought, he might surely make use of one of these.

'And they began to accuse him, saying: We have found this man

'(1) perverting our nation,
'(2) and forbidding to give tribute to Cæsar,
'(3) and saying he is Christ the King.'

With all his faults, perhaps because of his faults, Pilate had learnt much from experience. He had judged many a Jewish case before, and gained that power to distinguish reality from speciousness which the necessity for quick decision gives. He had no trouble to determine which of these three charges was the matter at stake. The first, that of 'perverting the Nation', he could set aside. Like the charge of being a 'malefactor', it was too vague to come within the Law. It was supported by no specific charge; for a matter of legal enquiry, there was need to state definitely something that the criminal had said or done, at some particular time and place. Nor need the second charge cause him much concern. If anyone had given trouble in the matter of taxes, it was these very men who were now crying out against this offender. Moreover, if there were any truth in what they said, he would have been in no need of their assistance to discover it; his carefully graded tax-collectors and his police would long since have unearthed him.

But the third charge was more serious. At least, grotesque though it must have appeared to Pilate from the first, it brought the accused man definitely within the censure of the Law. On some occasion, in some place, it was alleged that the criminal had said that He was a king; He was thereby charged with the crime, *Læsæ Majestatis*, what had been formerly known as *perduellio*. Such a charge, at this particular moment of Roman history, was perhaps the most serious that could be preferred against any man; with no other were the courts liable to be more severe, in no other case was injustice liable to be more common. In the days of the Republic the Laws *De majestate* had covered acts of disloyalty or injury to the Roman State; now they included, and indeed were most concerned with, acts against the Roman Emperor. He was the Empire, he was the impersonation of Rome, already his statue had begun to appear alongside those of the gods, and to be treated, like theirs, as something sacred. From the Emperor all authority came, on him all governors depended; to raise a standard against the Emperor was to challenge the whole Roman fabric, was a crime that would not be condoned.

Moreover, just at this period there were special reasons to keep a local governor on the alert. It was in the later days of Tiberius Cæsar, when security had made the Emperor careless and corrupt, and when tyranny flattered and humoured slavery, still citizens of Rome fancied themselves free. In his retirement at Capri, Tiberius was living his semblance of life, wearing himself out in a continual orgy. Secure against danger from without, he had entrusted all to his freedman, Sejanus; and Sejanus, whatever else he might condone, worked the Laws *De majestate* to their utmost limits. Under his rule never a word might be uttered against the sacred name of Cæsar, no laxity among the local governors would be condoned, as Pilate himself had already reason to know.

When, then, he heard the last accusation, that the criminal had declared Himself to be 'the king', however pitiful He seemed as He stood before His accusers, Pilate knew that, for his own sake, he could not pass the matter by; he must now go through the formalities and pass sentence, one way or the other. There must be the *citatio*; the accused must be brought in and questioned. In Rome, and in the greater Provinces, this was done by the *præco*, the *quæstor* appointed for the work. But in a smaller Province such as was Judæa, where the Governor had only a Procurator's rank and not that of a *Legatus*, the judge would call the accused man apart and examine him himself. The *citatio* is specially mentioned by St. John along with the words of the formal *interrogatio*:

'Pilate, therefore, went into the hall again, and called Jesus, and said to him: Art thou the king of the Jews?'

Thus from his seat of justice Pilate narrowed the case down to a single issue. Other charges he disregarded; even in the end he clung to this accusation and no other. Clearly the answer was both 'Yes' and 'No'; 'No' in the sense which alone concerned Pilate and the Roman Law; 'Yes' in the sense which alone affected the accusers. But Pilate thus far knew nothing of this second sense; a 'king', to him, had only one meaning. The accusers played upon his ignorance, as false accusers regularly do; they confounded the two meanings, thus turning truth into a lie, without the alteration of a single word. Again their cleverness had provided him with an escape if he chose to take it; if Pilate were wise he would find the man guilty and would condemn on this account, and ask no further questions.

But here, as always, their Victim was more than their equal, more even than the equal of the Judge who had cited and questioned Him. Pilate must be saved from the trap prepared for him; while Jesus would not yield one tittle of the truth, He must, nevertheless, protect His judge from any act of ignorant injustice. By a single assertion He made the distinction clear:

' Jesus answered: Sayest thou this thing of thyself, or have others told it thee of me ? '

It was as much as to say:

' Pilate, you are the Roman Governor. In your eyes, and in the eyes of the Roman Law, to assume the name of ' king ' is a challenge to Roman authority. But in the eyes of my accusers it means no such thing ; it has a meaning all its own. Do you then ask me as Roman Governor, or do you ask me to reply as I would reply to them ? '

It was a prisoner's honest and lawful defence ; at the same time it did not yield one step. The Governor was shown that the word ' king ' was being used in two senses, the first of which alone concerned him, as it alone came within the cognisance of the Roman Law. In that sense Jesus was innocent, and He was prepared to declare it ; but He would not declare it if by doing so He must surrender His title to the second. But this second sense concerned the Law of Moses, and was no affair of Pilate's ; it belonged to the ecclesiastical courts, where the scribes and Pharisees must settle matters for themselves. Pilate accepted the invitation.

' Pilate answered: Am I a Jew ? Thy nation and its chief priests have delivered thee up to me. What hast thou done ? '

So suddenly, yet so completely, had the tables been turned ; it was Pilate, not Christ, who was put on his defence. He was judge, not of Christ's Jewish claim, but of His claim as it affected Rome. If his prisoner repudiated the second, then why had His own nation, of whom He claimed to be king, delivered Him up to Roman Authority ? What had He done to deserve such handling ? The desire for a concrete charge, upon which a concrete sentence could be passed, characteristic of the Roman courts, was evident in the question.

The answer of Jesus was prompt. The judge had acknowledged the distinction, and that the second meaning of the word was of no interest to him ; Jesus could now speak of His Kingdom and His Kingship without fear of offending against the Roman Law. The judge had asked what He had done that He should have been brought to this pass. He would enlighten him; enough at least to make him sure that neither he, nor Tiberius, nor the Roman Empire had anything to fear from whatever authority He claimed. Nay, more, not even had His enemies anything to fear; if Pilate thought that by releasing Him he might do injury to His accusers, he might put himself at ease.

'Jesus answered: My kingdom is not of this world. If my kingdom were of this world my servants would certainly strive that I should not be delivered to the Jews: but now my kingdom is not from hence.'

Here was something new, Jesus was no king in the Roman sense; that had already been made clear. But now He claimed to be no king in the Jewish sense; He said that He had been 'delivered to the Jews', that His kingdom had nothing to do with the Jews or the Roman Province. Still less, then, did He come under sentence; there was nothing more that concerned him, either as judge or as Roman Governor. But something remained that concerned him as a man, and to satisfy himself he would ask a further question. In two senses Jesus had disclaimed the title of king; none the less, He had claimed a kingdom. Then in some other sense He must be a king. It was not as part of the trial, it was as man to man, that Pilate put the question once more:

'Pilate therefore said to him: Art thou a king then?'

Or, as it might be translated: 'So thou art a king after all?'

Was Pilate still manœuvring for position? Was this question that of the clever barrister's cross-examination, seeking to make the witness contradict himself? Was it a last effort to recover the command he had lost? If so, he might have spared his labour. Jesus had vindicated Himself on two possible charges, now He could speak 'as one having authority', even to the Roman judge, without any fear, either of committing Himself, or of being misunderstood:

'Jesus answered: Thou sayest that I am a king. For this I was born, and for this came I into the world, that I should give testimony to the truth. Every one that is of the truth heareth my voice.'

It was one of those answers of Jesus given at moments of crisis, not for the questioner only, but for all men and for all time. Pilate did not ignore that reply. He could, and under the circumstances naturally would, affect to ignore it; it was the only way to keep his place.

'Pilate saith to him: What is truth?'

But for the rest of that day he could not forget it. Jesus Christ was a true king; yet was He no king that Roman Law could condemn. Throughout the rest of that strange morning it rang in his ears and expressed itself in his words:

'You have brought this man to me as one that perverteth the people, and behold I, having examined him before you, find no cause in this man, touching these things wherein you accuse him.'

'You have a custom that I should release one unto you at the Pasch. Will you therefore that I release unto you the King of the Jews?'

'What will you, then, that I do with Jesus, that is called Christ, the King of the Jews?'

'Why, what evil hath he done? I find no cause of death in him. I will chastise him, therefore, and let him go.'

'I am innocent of the blood of this just man, look you to it.'

'Take him you and crucify him, for I find no cause in him.'

'Shall I crucify your king?'

'And Pilate wrote a title also, and he put it upon the cross over his head. And the writing was: This is Jesus of Nazareth, the King of the Jews.'

'Pilate answered: What I have written, I have written.'

'But Pilate wondered that he should be already dead.'

When we put these sentences together, we see plainly the working of Pilate's mind. From first to last there is no question of the kingship of Jesus in any Roman sense. But there *is* question of the kingship of the Jews; and to that Pilate clings to the end, no matter how often and how completely the Jewish leaders reject it. Jesus is a king, yet not in the sense of the scribes and Pharisees. Jesus does not deserve to die, yet must He be condemned. It is a living portrait of a judge beaten by fear, yet clinging always to this straw to save himself; on the one hand from the Jewish rabble and the Roman Cæsar, on the other from this king, this witness to the truth, this Son of God.

'We have a law; and according to that law he ought

to die, because he made himself the Son of God. When Pilate therefore had heard this saying he feared the more.'

This is no invented story ; it quivers with truth in every line. But we must return to the legal process. The *citatio* and *interrogatio* had taken place, and it had been found impossible to formulate a definite, unambiguous charge. There was nothing more to be done but to pronounce the sentence of acquittal: *Actore non probante, reus absolvitur.* Pilate went out on to the balcony and faced the accusers.

' And when he had said this he went forth again to the Jews, and said to them: I find no cause in him.'

From the side of Roman Law this was final. It remained only to clear the court, and set their prisoner free. But the court was not cleared, and the prisoner was not free ; and for the rest of that morning all law was thrown to the winds.

XII

JESUS, THE REVELATION OF GOD

'GOD, who at sundry times and in divers manners spoke, in times past, to the fathers by the prophets, last of all, in these days, hath spoken to us by his Son; whom he hath appointed heir of all things, by whom also he made the world. Who, being the brightness of his glory, and the figure of his substance, and upholding all things by the word of his power, making purgation of sins, sitteth on the right hand of the majesty on high' (Hebrews i, 1-3).

When we study the claim of Jesus Christ Our Lord and the significance of His revelation, we cannot make too much of this introduction to the Epistle to the Hebrews. The author is about to enter on the argument for Christ as it would most appeal to the Jewish mind, and, like a sound controversialist, he begins by stating what is common ground, and what every Jew of his generation will admit. He is not writing for an agnostic or a rationalistic age such as ours; he has no need to define his terms, like St. Paul before the Greeks. He can assume the fact of the one, true God, almighty, everlasting, the Lord of heaven and earth; Him whom his readers have always held to be peculiarly their own, the God of Israel. He can assume, moreover, as accepted by them all, the fact of Divine revelation; that God has chosen, at sundry times and by divers means, to make Himself and His ordinances known to His own people. He has sent to them prophets, and has spoken to them by their mouth; He has given certain signs, certain manifestations, by which they might know His mind and His will. As the centuries have succeeded one another, these prophecies and signs have accumulated; each has added something to their knowledge, each has encouraged them to believe that one day the picture would be com-

pleted, one day the coping-stone would be put to complete
the arch that spanned the history of the Jewish people.

Thus much he knows he can assume ; there will be no
faithful Jew who reads his argument, not even the most
perverse and obstinate, but will readily concede these two
postulates. Then, with a magnificent sweep characteristic
of St. Paul, he asserts in brief the thesis he is about to
maintain. This completion of the picture, for which they
have so long been looking, has at last in their own day
been accomplished ; the stone, though rejected by the
builders, has been set in its place and the arch has been
rounded. God has finally spoken, no longer by a prophet
but by His own Son ; and because He has so spoken His
message is now complete. He has spoken by One who is
His equal ; who reflects Him and His word perfectly ;
who, with Him, is the Creator and Lord of all that is ;
who with Him can purify from sin. He has revealed
Himself through One who is in the fullest sense Divine ;
who, having finished the work that was given to Him, has
returned to His rightful place in heaven, and sits now
on the right hand of the Father, above the prophets, above
the very angels, truly God and truly Man, 'a priest for
ever according to the order of Melchisedech ', ' ever living
to make intercession for us '

We say we cannot make too much of the assumption contained in this preface to the Epistle to the Hebrews,
because it expresses the background against which Jesus
and His revelation can alone be adequately judged. The
Jews of His time, one and all, good and bad, devout and
worldly minded, believed in the one true God of their
fathers, in the fact of successive revelation to their race,
in the promise that some day, and indeed in their day, the
Messias would come and complete all that had already
been revealed. If we take the Gospels as witness to their
times and no more, they are full of this belief and antici-
pation. The scenes that make up the story of the Nativity,
from the message to Zachary to the return of the Holy
Family to Nazareth, seem almost to have been selected to
emphasise this fact. When the Baptist appeared, again the
first question was whether or not he was the Messias ; and
that, not from his followers only, but from observant
critics in Jerusalem. When Jesus was at last manifested,
it was as the Messias that His first disciples welcomed
Him ; doubting followers of the Baptist chose this as

their test question ; until the very end His enemies complained that He would not make clear to them whether or not He was the Christ.

Upon a scene with a background such as this we see a man come from a hidden country village of Galilee, one more, it might have been thought, of the claimants to the title of Messias, and less plausible than many. And yet at once, by a kind of instinct, by a kind of apprehension, before He has yet spoken a word, men of goodwill begin to gather to Him, while those in high places in Jerusalem begin to watch and suspect Him. He makes no attempt to stir up a revolution ; He stands back as if He does not mind whether men follow Him or not. It is not, therefore, any political issue, any unwonted rousing of the people, whether against themselves or against their Roman overlords, that gives them their first cause for fear. He walks in amongst them regardless of their animosity, as a king might walk through his own palace. He acts singlehanded, on His own authority, without a follower to support Him, and they stand by Him stupefied, paralysed, not knowing what they shall say or do. They do not treat Him as they would treat any other man who did the like, and as any disturber of the peace should be treated, with contempt and the hand of the Law. They know at once that here is something new ; that in this Man who so reveals Himself there is a tremendous challenge. They ask Him for His credentials, His testimonials, His right to act as He did ; by their very demand they acknowledge Him as their Master from the first.

When at length He begins to speak, it is not so much the substance of His teaching that troubles them ; it is the constant challenge of the Man Himself. They are the masters in Israel, the expounders of the Law and the Prophets, and none would dare to set himself up as equal to any one of them. But this Man from Nazareth, who ' has never learnt ', puts His word above that of Moses. He declares their God-given Law to be imperfect, and that He has come to perfect it. He gives a new meaning to the prophecies by claiming to fulfil them in Himself. He does not argue tentatively as do the scribes ; He speaks in public and in private, as one who had authority to speak. Man though He showed Himself at every point, yet He speaks of Himself as exalted above all creatures. Nay, more, He puts Himself on the level of God Himself, demanding from men implicit faith, entire love, and even allowing men to fall down and worship Him. Sometimes He would induce men to it, as with a blind beggar, whom He healed in the city of Jerusalem. He claims to forgive sins, which He allows that only God can do, and to prove His claim He raises a paralytic from his bed. What prophet before Him had ever dreamt of doing that ? The Pharisees were right in their conclusion: either Jesus had that power or He had not ; either He was equal to God or what He said was blasphemy.

But that was by no means all. From the first the charge was brought against Him that 'He made Himself the Son of God' ; and that in a sense literal and true, in a sense that meant for Him the same obeisance as was given to the Father in heaven. 'Amen, amen, I say to thee that we speak what we 'know, and we testify what we have seen' (John iii, 11). 'All things are delivered to me by my father. And no one knoweth the Son but the Father —and who the Father is, but the Son, and to whom the Son will reveal him' (Luke x, 22). 'This is the will of my Father, that every one who seeth the Son and believeth in him may have everlasting life, and I will raise him up in the last day' (John vi, 40). As time went on, claims and declarations such as these multiplied, in Jerusalem where they could not be mistaken, in Galilee where their meaning grew upon a less sophisticated people. 'You are from beneath, I am from above. You are of this world, I am not of this world' (John viii, 23). 'Before Abraham was made I am' (John viii, 58). 'I and the Father are one' (John x, 30). 'Thou art Christ, the Son of the living God' (Matt. xvi, 16). 'And now glorify thou me, O Father, with thyself, with the glory which I had, before the world was, with thee' (John xvii, 5). We watch the revelation growing in emphatic clearness, to His friends and to His enemies, until the climax is reached: 'I adjure thee by the living God, that thou tell us if thou be the Christ the Son of God' (Matt. xxvi, 63). 'He hath blasphemed. What further need have we of witnesses ? ' (ibid, 65). 'We have a law, and according to the Law he ought to die, because he made himself the Son of God' (John xix, 7). Messias, Son of Man, true Son of God ; there is no mistaking the development, consistent from the first, without any groping or hesitation of His own. He goes straight forward to His goal, training men, friends and enemies, to follow Him, knowing well all the time that He was 'set for the fall and for the resurrection of many', that because some would not take it He must die, but for those who would, it was eternal life.

If He was thus clear and emphatic in His witness of Himself before men, no less was His witness confirmed by His dealing with God, His Father. It is that of a true Son with a true Father, of a loving Son, who has the service of His Father always before His eyes, who has no other object in life. 'Did you not know that I must be about my Father's business ?' (Luke ii, 49), are the first words we hear that He uttered ; and they are the motto of His whole career. 'The Father in heaven, My Father, Your Father, Our Father' ; He can never speak of God but He must give Him this name, and that with all the affection of a son who is keen that all should know the length and breadth of that Father's love. Into the hands of the Father, in life and in death, He surrendered His all: 'My meat is to do the will of him that sent me' (John iv, 34). He had no other object in life: 'I do always the things that please him' (John viii, 29) ; He had no other satisfaction but the knowledge that the Father was well pleased: 'At the same hour he rejoiced in the Holy Ghost and said: I confess to thee, O Father, Lord of heaven and earth, because thou hast hid these things from the wise and prudent, and hast revealed them to little ones. Yea, Father, for so it hath seemed good in thy sight' (Luke x, 21). If even His own deserted Him, still He was 'not alone, for the Father is in me' ; if the burden was apparently too much for Him, nevertheless: 'Father, not as I will, but as thou wilt' (Matt. xxvi, 39) ; when at last the hour of death came: 'Father, into thy hands I commend my spirit' (Luke xxiii, 46). Throughout His life we are impressed by that familiarity, that intimacy, that natural tendency to prayer which is certainly His first human characteristic, and which gradually grew upon His own till in the end they saw in prayer the best imitation of their Master.

'We have found the Messias ; we have found him of whom Moses in the Law and the prophets did write.' If this could be said by a disciple on the day of their first meeting, what would he have said at the end ? It was the same disciple who at the Last Supper said: 'Lord, show us the Father, and it is enough for us' (John xiv, 8). But indeed he had been shown the Father. For when next we come to consider what was the message the Son of God had brought from heaven, is it too much to say that it was precisely this: the revelation of the Fatherhood of God ? By this alone, as someone has said, the religion of Jesus was really a new thing. To whom had this intimate affection of God occurred before ? Even in the psalms He was the King, to be adored and loved as by a servant ; the service and love of a child was scarcely there. To the Jews in the centuries He had always been the Judge, just, merciful, forgiving, worthy of all love ; nevertheless the idea that He was what Jesus claimed for Him would have seemed almost blasphemy. Yet it was precisely this that Jesus emphasised. He did not depart from the teaching of the prophets. God was still 'Lord of heaven and earth', man was still His servant ; but Jesus added this new thing, the Fatherhood with all it entailed. The Jews might begin their morning prayer with the words: 'Praise be to thee, Lord, our God and the God of our Fathers' ; He would have His disciples begin: 'Our Father who art in heaven'. This gave a new orientation. The Father who was in heaven would give good things to them that asked Him. Let them not think too much what they should eat nor what they should drink, for their Father knew they had need of these things. Let them not be afraid for it had pleased their Father to give them a Kingdom. Let them love, not only 'the Lord their God', but Him who loved them as a Father. There is immense significance in that final prayer of Jesus: 'Father, I have manifested thy name '—the name of Father —'to the men whom thou hast given me. Holy Father, keep them in thy name. Just Father, the world hast not known thee, but I have known thee. And I have made known thy name to them, and will make it known, that the love wherewith thou hast loved me may be in them, and I in them (John xvii). We do not wonder that those who came after Him seized upon this as the centre of all. 'I write unto you, babes, because you have known the Father', writes St. John (1 John ii, 14) ; and he points to the highest goal a little later: 'Behold what manner of charity the Father hath bestowed upon us that we should be called and should be the sons of God ; Dearly beloved, we are now the sons of God ; and it hath not yet appeared what we shall be' (1 John iii, 1, 2). And St. Paul, con-

trasting the old with the new: 'You have not received the
spirit of bondage in fear: but have received the spirit of
adoption of sons, whereby we cry: Abba Father. For the
Spirit himself giveth testimony to our spirit that we are
the sons of God. And if sons, heirs also: heirs indeed of
God, and co-heirs with Christ' (Romans viii, 15-17).

Next, with the teaching of the Fatherhood of God there
came the proclaiming of the Father's Kingdom. The
'sons of God', the sons of such a Father, were not human
beings and no more ; they were princes of His household,
who were to sit at His table, and were to rule as the
Father would give them to rule. 'Thy kingdom come'
was to be on their lips when they spoke to their Father, as
if that were to be the happy consummation of all things
in this weary world ; a kingdom not indeed of this world
as had been expected, though it was to be intimately
within it, as the leaven in the bread ; a spiritual kingdom,
but one that gave life, a kingdom of grace and truth ; a
kingdom of free men, yes, but freed essentially from sin,
of victorious men, but conquerors mainly of themselves.
It was a kingdom of a new chosen people, that would
come from east and west, to be preached to every creature,
whether Gentile or Jew ; a kingdom to be entered by a
new initiation, by faith in Himself, Jesus Christ, its King,
and by the baptism that He ordained. The founding of
that Kingdom would be the turning-point in the history
of mankind ; it would be a treasure of great price which
he who discovered it would value above all things else. In
time to come men would see that kingdom, as a city on a
hill, as a festival board toward which all eyes would turn.
It would be built upon a rock and nothing would prevail
against it ; it would be founded in the hearts of men and
no power on earth or in hell would be able to eradicate it.
It would grow as a tree from a seed till it covered the
whole earth ; it would spread as leaven in bread, till the
whole race of men was leavened by it. It would suffer
violence, yet would never perish ; its children would
suffer, yet in the midst of their suffering their sorrow
would be turned into joy. Such would be its story in this
world ; at the end would be its perfect fulfilment, in
itself and for all its members: 'Come, ye blessed of my
Father, possess the kingdom prepared for you from the
beginning of the world'.

Not only was God the Father of men, not only were

His children destined to be princes in His Kingdom, in
this world and in the next ; God was also the standard
of all life, the ideal toward which every child of His Kingdom might aspire. ' Be you therefore perfect, as your
heavenly Father is perfect ' (Matt. v, 48), was uttered as
a new thing early in the life of Jesus ; it remained
implicit till the end. ' Be ye holy, because I am holy '
(Lev. xi, 44), had been said in the Law of Moses ; here
was an ideal that was far more intimate. Away, then,
with those external standards and signs of holiness which
had been sufficient for scribes and Pharisees ; the washing of hands, the avoidance of sinners, the outward observance of the sabbath, the straining out of gnats and
swallowing camels, the ' heavy and insupportable burdens '
which were for ever being multiplied and laid on men's
shoulders. Instead, Jesus would have men be holy ' unseen
by men ', judge of justice from within. If the heart were
evil, no external cleansing could save it ; if the heart were
good and true, purification without mattered little.
Sanctity was not to be measured by what men might see
and think about it ; it was what it was in the sight of the
Father and no more. ' Thou, when thou shalt pray, enter
into thy chamber, and, having shut the door, pray to thy
Father in secret. And thy Father, who seeth in secret,
will repay thee ' (Matt. vi, 6). ' God knoweth your
hearts, for that which is high to men is an abomination
before God ' (Luke xvi, 15). Likeness to the Father, the
source and centre of all good ; intimacy with the Father,
who held His own near to His heart ; a child's love and
service of the Father, simple, and confident, and entire ;
from that a child's love of all the Father loved, whether
good or bad, friends or enemies: ' On these two commandments dependeth the whole Law and the prophets '
(Matt. xxii, 40). To this all the rest was relative and no
more ; from it all the rest drew whatever of good was
in it.

' On these two commandments ' depended all the rest ;
this was a new thing and the last. He Himself had demon-
strated this in all He had said and done ; in His blessing
on the poor and meek, in His gentleness alike to His
friends and His enemies, in His invincible forgivingness
no matter what men might do to Him: ' Judas, dost thou
betray the Son of Man ? ' (Luke xxii, 48). ' Jesus turning
looked on Peter ' (Luke xxii, 61). ' Father, forgive them,

for they know not what they do' (Luke xxiii, 34). He had shown it in His fathomless compassion for the leper on the road, for the widow bereaved, for two sisters who mourned a dead brother, for the whole multitude that was distressed, 'and lying like sheep that had no shepherd' (Matt. ix, 36). He had drawn on those who loved Him to love others for His sake, saying that what they did to them they did to Him: 'Amen, I say to you, as long as you did it to one of these my least brethren, you did it to me' (Matt. xxv, 40). At the end of all, as if to sum up all He had taught in one word, He reiterated this as a 'new commandment', as the one sign by which His disciples would be known, as the one thing above all things else in which they should take Him as their model: 'A new commandment I give unto you: that you love one another as I have loved you, that you also love one another. By this shall all men know that you are my disciples, if you have love one for another' (John xiii, 34, 35). In this He would have the contrast proved between the Old and the New: 'You have heard that it hath been said, thou shalt love thy neighbour and hate thy enemy. But I say to you, love your enemies, do good to them that hate you, and pray for them that persecute and calumniate you' (Matt. v, 43, 44). Indeed, as if His message should be rounded off, and end where it had begun, in doing this they would prove themselves 'children of the Father, who maketh his sun to rise upon the good and the bad, and raineth upon the just and the unjust' (Matt. v, 45). The message of Jesus Christ is transcendentally a message of love.

These were the 'good tidings of great joy to all the people' which Jesus gave to the world; greater than any other that had ever been given before, unequalled by any teaching since, more than natural in spite of their utter simplicity. And all this He confirmed, emphasised, placed beyond question, or argument, or doubt, by the intense, convincing personality manifested in Himself. We may look back and may see that there was knowledge in Him more than that possessed by any man, knowledge of this world and of the next; truth, infallibility, in regard to the present and to the future, explaining that 'speaking with authority' which convinced His hearers, though they could not have said why. We look at Him and recognise His absolute sinlessness, so secure that He could defy His

enemies to convince Him of any sin ; no man before Him
or since, be he ever so perfect, has been able, or has
ventured to do that. We listen to Him, and there rings
out in every word that absolute truthfulness which even
His enemies allowed to Him: 'Master, we know that
thou art a true speaker and teachest the way of God in
truth ' (Matt. xxii, 16). We watch Him and marvel at
His bravery in facing every ordeal, His humility in re-
maining always as other men, His gentleness in manner
that made Him always all things to all, His compassion
for all suffering, His abiding, invincible love of His fellow-
men, even of His enemies, so that however He might be
compelled to rebuke them yet never could anyone complain that he had been slighted, or condemned, or insulted. ' He is a good man ', said the people in the Temple
when they discussed Him (John vii, 12) ; ' He hath done
all things well ', cried the crowds in Decapolis ; ' He went
about doing good ' (Acts x, 38), was the summary of His
life when He had gone and all was over. St. Paul expresses it with greater force ; to him the whole life of
Jesus was ' the appearance of the love and kindness of
God our Saviour ' (Titus iii, 4) ; His life was in itself the
manifestation of God.

Indeed, Jesus Christ spoke with justice when He said
that He was, with His Father, His own witness. ' Although I give testimony of myself, my testimony is true '
(John viii, 14). On the evidence of His own life, and of
all that has come to the world because of Him, He was
the greatest of men, He was too great to be merely man,
He was Divine, He was what He declared Himself to be,
the Divine and the human were united in His Person,
He was the true Son of God. Let us get out of our
self-conscious, sophisticated, windy generation, and the
truth appears ; judge Him in Himself, and by the
standards of a generation that was alive, and which put
Him to every test, and we cannot make any mistake. He
is absolute, He is perfect, He is universal ; He is free
from the limitations of common men, He is of every time,
of every generation, He stands alone ; there is none to
compare with Him, even the saints who have come after
Him, and have moulded their lives on His example, fall
far behind Him in perfection, remain feeble men like the
rest. He inspired hatred as no other man, love as no other,
and to this day that hatred and that love have remained ;

of what other man, in all the world's history, can even a semblance of this be said ? No man has influenced the world as He has influenced it ; no man in any generation affected it as He ; to-day no name stands for more throughout the world than the undying, all-winning Name of Jesus Christ. And it is the living Person that had had that influence, far more than what He said and did ; though what He said and did stand for more in the making of the world than all the words and all the deeds of all sages and philosophers combined. Men revere Him to-day, and the reverence never wearies or grows less. They admire Him with an enthusiasm that can be given to no dead thing ; they love Him, they serve Him, with a love and a service they could give to no other. Indeed He is His own witness, and the confession lives on: ' Thou art Christ, the Son of the living God ' (Matt. xvi, 16).

In all that has been said hitherto we have made little reference to the works by which Jesus Christ gave proof of the power that was in Him. Yet, when everything else failed to convince His enemies, He Himself appealed to these as a final argument. ' Though you will not believe me ', He said, ' believe the works ' (John x, 38), for these ' give testimony of me ' (John v, 36). The miracles of Jesus Christ have their importance, and that chiefly in this, that they are unique. Others have worked miracles before Him and since ; He told His disciples that they should do greater things than He did. But they have worked them, not in their own name, not by any power of their own. Jesus alone claims power as essentially belonging to Himself ; He alone works miracles by His own word: if others should work them it would be ' in His name ', by power which He would delegate to them. In this He showed Himself the Lord of all the world, of the things of earth, of nature ˌitself, of life and death, of the very powers that were outside nature ; His word was the word of the Almighty, who made all things, who created all things, and could unmake or change as He had made. ' All things were made by him, and without him was made nothing that was made ' (John i, 3). ' I will, be thou made clean ' (Matt. viii, 3). ' Young man, I say to thee, arise ' (Luke vii, 14). ' Receive thy sight ' (Luke xviii, 42). ' Lazarus, come forth ' (John xi, 43). ' I have power to lay down my life, and take it up again ' (John x, 18). There is a witness in the manner of all these that cannot be gainsaid, except by the flattest refusal to accept all evidence. It is easier to ignore a miracle worked before our very eyes than to set aside the authority and the deeds of Him who spoke and acted with such supreme right. Peter could later say: 'In the name of Jesus Christ of Nazareth, arise and walk' (Acts iii, 6); Jesus acted in His own name. It is not the nature of the miracle itself which matters, it is the manner of Him who worked it. Unbelief has endeavoured to explain away the first, the second it has merely ignored.

But of nothing is this more true than of the crowning miracle of all, the raising by Jesus of His own body from the dead. Repeatedly He had said that He would do it; he was yet alive: After three days I will rise again' (Matt. xxvii, 63). Of the permanent belief in the fact, give other meanings to His words, they showed at the end that they understood full well what He had meant: 'Sir, we have remembered that that seducer said, while he was yet alive: After three days I will rise again' (Matt. xxvii, 63). Of the permanent belief in the fact, fixed firm and proclaimed in the open streets from within fifty days of the event, and within a few hundred yards of the open grave, we have ample evidence; of the persistence of that belief, simple and entire and without equivocation, the whole story of the Early Church bears witness. 'Witnesses of the Resurrection' (cf. Acts i, 22); this was the title of the Twelve; they were witnesses to men who were not fools or enthusiasts, but subtle Greeks and sober-minded Romans, yet they won their way. Those who would deny the Resurrection have a mighty task before them. They must not only explain the empty tomb, which was there for anyone to explore; they must not only account for the silence of the scribes and Pharisees, who might easily have produced counter-evidence if it were there. They may not merely say that Peter 'was full of new wine' (Acts ii, 13); they must find a cause for that abiding certainty upon which the whole faith of Christianity has been built, and for which the millions have died. 'If Christ be not risen, then is our faith vain' (1 Cor. xv, 14), proclaimed St. Paul, relying with confidence on the firm knowledge of those who heard him. To believe in such a thing demanded a faith more than human from the first, yet was that faith freely given. It had the evidence of experience against it, no less then than now, men could say then, as they say to-day, that the dead do not rise ; yet that faith persisted and never flinched. The wisdom of Jewry found it a stumbling-block ; to the philosophic Gentile it was merely foolish ; none the less did those who knew hold to it, declaring it the power and the glory of God. They held to it, and to Him who had thereby proved Himself Master of life and death, of this world and the next, of time and eternity. And in that faith they had looked into the future, and prophesied what would be with a confidence that has no parallel. 'Having risen, he dieth no more ; death shall no more have dominion over him' (Rom. vi, 9). He had made one promise, that He would do what no man could do, and He had kept His word ; He had made another, again beyond the power of any man, and He would keep that no less. 'Behold, I am with you all days, even to the consummation of the world' (Matt. xxviii, 20). In the strength of that assurance they had gone forth to the conquest of mankind, and even to this day, 'Behold, all the world goes after them' (John xii, 19). All this they must needs explain who would deny the Resurrection of Our Lord Jesus Christ: 'Yesterday, to-day, and the same for ever' (Heb. xiii, 8).

THE END

Made in the USA
Monee, IL
09 August 2022

11215156R00095